Praise for B

'An all-in-one reference to an array of issues in the primary school.'

Laura Kennedy, classroom teacher

'As with all of Kevin's writing, this book is clever, funny, informative and written from his experience as a Brilliant Teacher and Brilliant Headteacher. I wish someone had given me this book when I was a Probationer (as we called NQTs in 1978). It could have saved me a lot of time and a lot of embarrassment and I'd have had a lot more fun a whole lot earlier.'

Sheila Young, District Education Manager, New Forest, Hants.

'This book is well structured, easy to follow and full of practical 'brilliant' tips. It is refreshing to read a book which highlights real and challenging issues for new staff at the same time as offering so many suggestions for success. Kevin offers scenarios which are useful not only for the individual reader but also as a resource for school training activities. This book reminds the teacher or new leader that they are human and looking after themselves is as important as looking after others. The question about the legacy one wants to leave is important for all teachers and Kevin's book with humour and humanity gives interesting perspectives and love for the profession.'

Carolyn Hughan, Leadership Adviser, Hampshire Teaching and Learning College

'A very informative, supportive resource with plenty of practical guidance for both newly qualified and experienced teachers. The author has created a wealth of advice that you'll want to revisit time and time again.'

Mike Earle, Key Stage 2 Manager

'Kevin's cutting-edge but no-nonsense approach to school leadership shines through in this book. He is not afraid to talk about the tricky issues of school life, and his writing is packed full of top tips for surviving teaching and implementing those high ideals without sacrificing work-life balance. This, along with Kevin's dry sense of humour interspersed throughout, makes for a refreshing read.'

Alison Lockwood, Deputy Headteacher, Crofton Hammond Infants School, Stubbington

Brilliant series list

brilliant

primary school teacher

What you need to know to be a truly outstanding teacher

Kevin Harcombe

Prentice Hall
is an imprint of

PEARSON

Harlow, England • London • New York • Boston • San Francisco • Toronto • Sydney • Singapore • Hong Kong
Tokyo • Seoul • Taipei • New Delhi • Cape Town • Madrid • Mexico City • Amsterdam • Munich • Paris • Milan

PEARSON EDUCATION LIMITED

Edinburgh Gate
Harlow CM20 2JE
Tel: +44 (0)1279 623623
Fax: +44 (0)1279 431059
Website: www.pearsoned.co.uk

First published in Great Britain in 2011

ISBN: 978–0–273–73250–1

British Library Cataloguing-in-Publication Data
A catalogue record for this book is available from the British Library

Library of Congress Cataloging-in-Publication Data
Harcombe, Kevin.
  Brilliant primary school teacher : what you need to know to be a truly outstanding teacher / Kevin Harcombe.
     p. cm.
  ISBN 978-0-273-73250-1 (pbk.)
  1. Elementary school teacher. 2. Effective teaching. 3. Elementary school teachers--Professional relationships. I. Title
   LB1555.H287 2011
   372.1102--dc22

                                        2011002662

10 9 8 7 6 5 4 3 2 1
15 14 13 12 11

Typeset in 10/14pt Plantin Regular by 3
Printed and bound in Great Britain by Henry Ling Ltd, Dorchester, Dorset

Contents

Foreword

This is a timely and massively important publication.

Education is the answer to all the challenges we face today – personally and socially, locally and globally. As Nelson Mandela put it, 'Education is the most powerful weapon we have to change the world.' It is the key to the myriad economic, environmental, medical, cultural and technological issues that will frame our lives in future – and it is teachers who hold the key to education.

Our children deserve nothing less than the best – the brightest, most brilliant teachers on the planet – because, in Sir Michael Barber's words, 'The quality of an education system cannot exceed the quality of its teachers'. And of all the important members of the teaching profession, primary teachers are arguably the most important, because the sooner you make a difference in a child's life, the more radical the transformation can be.

So this book is timely, and utterly essential reading for all primary teachers and all prospective primary teachers.

There are few people better qualified than Kevin Harcombe to write about what makes a brilliant primary teacher. On the recommendation of his community and peers – including other outstanding teachers and headteachers – and in recognition of his exceptional work, he was awarded a UK Teaching Award in 2007. He knows how to inspire and engage children, as is evident from the achievements of children in his school. Perhaps more importantly, when our judges visited the school, children queued up to sing his praises.

Kevin has consistently made a difference to the lives of the children he works with: he knows what it takes to be a brilliant teacher and he can show you what it takes to be one. Don't take my word for it. Read on and find out for yourself.

Caroline Evans
Chief Executive
The Teaching Awards

List of terms and abbreviations

ADHD	attention deficit hyperactivity disorder
AfL	Assessment for Learning
APP	Assessing Pupil Progress
CPD	continuing professional development
CPLO	child protection liaison officer sometimes now known as the designated person for child protection
CRB	Criminal Records Bureau
DCSF	Department for Education
DPCP	designated person for child protection – still often referred to as child protection liaison officer
DT	design technology
G&T	gifted and talented
H&S	health and safety
HMI	Her Majesty's Inspectorate
IEP	individual education plan
IT	information technology
ICT	information computer technology
IWB	interactive white board
KS1	Key Stage 1
KS2	Key Stage 2
NQT	newly qualified teacher
Ofsted	Office for Standards in Education
PGCE	post graduate certificate in education
PPA	planning, preparation and assessment
PTA	parent teacher association
PV	pupil voice

SATs	Standard Assessment Tests / Tasks
SEN	special educational needs
SENCO	special educational needs coordinator
SMART	specific measurable achievable realistic time-limited
TA	teaching assistant
TES	Times Educational Supplement
USP	unique selling point
VLE	virtual learning environment
VAK	visual aural kinaesthetic
WOWO	write on/wipe off

To my mother and father, my first brilliant teachers

Introduction

Too late!

If you are reading this you are probably already hooked.

You may be a primary teacher already, possibly even a brilliant one, taking an idly curious look at what *someone else* thinks constitutes brilliance. You may be doing initial teacher training and hoping to land your first job, or newly qualified and perhaps struggling to cope with that difficult first year. You may even be a teacher nearing the end of a career and checking out if I've included everything you hold dear.

You are unlikely to be a high-flying fat cat banker ('Daddy, what's a cat banker?') but, if you are (or if you're an accountant, stockbroker, single mum, dad, soldier, shopkeeper), already you are interested enough to be spending your precious time finding out what being a brilliant primary school teacher might entail.

At this stage, you need to know only one thing: being a primary school teacher probably is the best job in the world.

'But what about a prime minister or president? Astronaut, footballer, rock star or super model?' you might ask, in a sad attempt to join in my audience participation section.

The thing about prime ministers and the rest is they all had teachers. Teachers who saw or unearthed that spark in them, nurtured it and gave them the power to dream and to achieve. Teachers, without whom, they might never have succeeded in their chosen course. As a primary school teacher you will have the chance positively to enhance and enrich the life chances of several hundred fellow humans. You may never get to walk on the moon, strut down the catwalk to a million flashbulbs or score the injury time winner in a cup final – but you may enable others to do so. You will have passed on your values and your interests and enthusiasms and you will have made the world a better place.

The celebrated TV dramatist Jimmy McGovern (responsible for *Cracker*, *The Street* and many others) once revealed in an interview how his junior school teacher, Miss McCallum, inspired him to write and read, despite his pronounced stammer which frustrated and embarrassed him. I knew exactly what he meant, because Miss McCallum taught me too – in an inner city school where the children had nothing except the possibility of falling into the hands of a brilliant teacher. *You* could be a brilliant teacher for your children. *You* could inspire the next great writer or entrepreneur or doctor. *You* could nurture a successful plumber or builder through their initial faltering attempts at maths. In short, *you* could have the power to help shape the next generation. That's why, as the saying goes, 'Everyone remembers a brilliant teacher.'

They could remember *you*.

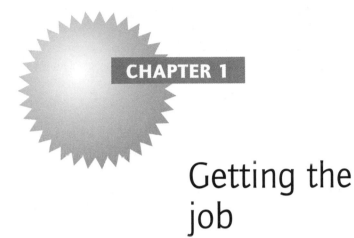

CHAPTER 1

Getting the job

I n this chapter we learn what the professional expectations of a teacher are and how to succeed at interview.

You may have seen something called the professional standards for teachers (http://www.tda.gov.uk/upload/resources/pdf/s/standards_a4.pdf). This sets out what you need to be a 'competent' class-based teacher. There are 41 sub headings, no more, no less, and it is, undoubtedly, the result of several long, dull, but worthy, committee meetings somewhere in a government building. They are worth a look, despite being couched in the sort of opaque, uninspiring language that committees use. If you are a new teacher, you need to look at the core standards in particular, which is where you should be at the end of your induction year.

Relationships with children and young people (C1) tops the list. You need to have high expectations of them, according to the standards. This isn't as obvious as it sounds. For a long time my school had a delightful ethos, which was caring and safe, but standards refused to budge from their low base. It was because, I found in a 'eureka!' moment, teachers' expectations of the children simply were not high enough. Perhaps they over compensated for the children's relatively deprived backgrounds. Perhaps they believed mistakenly that being sympathetic was more important than being challenging. Helping children to achieve as highly as they can, thereby giving them the means to live a happy, fulfilling and successful life, is what brilliant primary teaching should be

> never forget we are
> there to help them
> to learn as well as
> they can

about. That's why the nice people at the local authority pay our wages. That is our core purpose. Safeguard and care for children, but never forget we are there to help them to learn as well as they can.

Positive attitudes and values and high standards of professional behaviour (C2) is next – so stub out the fag, stop moaning about pay/children/the smoking ban and conduct yourself impeccably. This does not mean sainthood and restraint in your private life. Teachers love to party, and rightly so – just don't post the photos on Facebook for your class to see. You are a role model and how you talk to children is how they'll talk to others. The behaviours you model in school are the behaviours that they will hold in high regard. If you have a passion for reading, music or sport, the likelihood is that you will transmit some of that passion to them. Similarly, if you are a curmudgeonly misanthrope, don't be surprised if they absorb and reflect that too. (No one ever said this was easy!)

Communication and collaboration with all sections of the school community (C4–6) follows. Information should be 'timely and relevant', which rules out reporting in Year 6 that Freya has been dyslexic since Year 1 but 'she has a lovely smile'. Which brings me to parents. They may be antagonistic, demanding, rude, unreasonable, time-consuming and ungrateful. And they're just the good ones. The one golden rule to remember in dealing with parents is the huge emotional investment they have in their child – no matter that their child might be the most sullen, stubborn and ill mannered of all god's creatures. No matter that they might devote, in some instances, little time or care in their upbringing. The child is theirs and you need to remember that in all your dealings with them. Ask yourself, 'How would I feel if someone said or wrote this about a child of mine?' Always be honest, but don't always be frank. Never hide an unpalatable truth, but always look for the good as well – we all need hope, even if you might not think it deserved. More on parents in a later chapter.

Next comes *Personal and professional development* (C7–9), the nub of which is 'stand still and you'll go backwards'. The minute you stop developing and growing is the minute you cease to be effective. Being able and prepared to adapt is one hallmark of an outstanding teacher. Being open to innovation (which doesn't mean recklessly jumping on every crackpot bandwagon that hurtles down the educational highway) and wanting to learn to be the best teacher you can be are essential attributes. Openness and willingness to act on advice are prerequisites – but don't be uncritical. If an inspector or a headteacher is trying to convince you of the merits of a new initiative – perhaps Indian head massage for Year 3, or the importance of aromatherapy in maths lessons – they should be able to do just that: convince you. Never be afraid to question the benefits for the children.

Professional knowledge and understanding (C10–25) is the bread and butter stuff – being up to date, adaptable and selective in the strategies you use. The pre-eminence of formative assessment (often now referred to as AfL or assessment for learning) and the use of tracking data are rightly given emphasis. Safeguarding (number one in the Ofsted framework) and understanding diversity are also in there. Being up to date is vital (remember 'stand still, go backwards') whether through staff meetings (if they're good) in-school training or external courses, reading a professional journal and the like. But, appearing in several sections, AfL is the one to get right, for that will reap greater rewards for the children than anything else. AfL is the key to personalisation, reflective learning and high standards of attainment and achievement.

Professional skills (C26 onwards) deals with planning and design and the requirement to teach 'engaging and motivating lessons

... designed to raise levels of achievement', just when you were planning to teach a dull and demotivating lesson to make the children more stupid. Building on prior knowledge – i.e. not wasting time teaching children stuff they already know – and modifying your teaching to suit the needs of the learners (formerly known as differentiation) also loom large. Hands up if you've worked out that this is all related back to AfL? Told you it was important!

Assessing, monitoring and giving feedback (C31–34) – those government committee people know how to come up with a pithy, sexy title, don't they? This is, though, a little gem and C33 deserves quoting in full: 'Support and guide learners so that they can reflect on their learning, identify the progress they have made, set positive targets for improvement and become successful independent learners.' If you can achieve that – giving children the intrinsic capacity and desire to learn and reflect – you will have recorded a potentially great life-changing achievement for the child concerned. When you're at an interview and they ask, 'What would you lie down in the road for in education terms?', simply reply 'C33'. Of course, they'll never have heard of the reference C33 so you will have to explain it patiently to them before they offer you the job.

Reviewing teaching and learning (C35–36) – just as you always need to reflect on your own performance (and we all do rubbish lessons occasionally), so do learners need to reflect on theirs. The point of reflection is that you, and they, do it better next time.

Learning environment and managing behaviour (C38–39) – the learning environment is much more than the way you arrange the tables and the computerised, automated, coloured-pencil-rotating system you have worked out to prevent persistent cries of, 'Miss, Ahmed won't share the blue with me!' It is about that, but also about ethos and attitude and 'feel'. It is about how you relate to the children and how they relate to you, which brings me on to maintaining a 'clear and positive framework for discipline, in line with the school's behaviour policy' – which is sometimes easier said than done and will be dealt with in more detail later. *At this point, two absolutely vital messages will suffice.* First, if your lesson is pitched at an appropriate level and is interesting and engaging, many behaviour problems will not emerge. Second, always look to catch a child being good and praise them for it lavishly and specifically. 'Well done!' is not enough. 'Ashleigh, the way you worked out that problem using the number line was absolutely fantastic,' or 'Mustafa, you are working so hard to get this right, I'm really impressed with you!' This does not come naturally to some teachers. Try it. Watch the child swell with pride and work even harder.

Having acquainted yourself with the national standards, had a lie down and a cup of tea, you are now aware of the full extent of the task before you. You are also beginning to be equipped with the essential knowledge to go out, get that job and start enriching children's lives.

Job hunting

The colleges of education and universities are turning out better and better teachers. Competition for places is greater than it ever has been. So how do you ensure that you stand out from the crowd?

brilliant tip

Always, always, always visit a school you are thinking of applying to. Always visit when children are there. Clearly, if you are living in Cumbria and the school is in Cornwall, that might not be a practical proposition, but you can research it in other ways. Do your homework – view the website, read the Ofsted report (though these can quickly become out-of-date – good and bad – especially if there has been a change of head).

Make your application stand out from a pile of 70 – for good reasons, not for the spelling mistakes!

Show your individuality and talents in your personal statement – no one else is going to sell you, you have to do it yourself; this is not a time for hiding lights under bushels (whatever bushels might be).

Find out what the school is looking for. If the application details include a person specification, make sure your statement is geared to meet it, maybe even using their headings as headings for your statement. Never exaggerate to the extent that you will be found out. If they are looking for a musician, don't claim to be a virtuoso flautist if you can play only 'Row, row, row your boat'. On recorder. Badly.

The idea is to make it as easy as possible for the long listing group (reading 100 different applications that actually all look the same) to pick you out. Do their work for them and very likely it will pay off.

Make sure your referees know they will be approached. Nothing is guaranteed to make me grumpy more than receiving a reference request (usually three sides of tick-box hell) for someone who hasn't had the decency to ask me first.

If you email your application (increasingly the norm), request a read receipt to reassure yourself it's got there. Apart from that, don't badger the school to see how the application is progressing.

The application form: 10 ways to avoid the 'no' pile.

1 Get someone who knows what they're doing to proofread your application – when you're faced with dozens, the ones with spelling and grammar mistakes get ditched.

2 Include practical examples of what you have done, rather than copying chunks of bland teaching philosophy from some website.

3 What is your unique selling point (USP) – that distinguishes your application from all the others? Get it in.

4 Never write more than the two sides of A4 allotted and don't use a ridiculously miniscule font. Some of the best forms I've seen have been only one to one and a half sides long. It's *what* you write rather than *how much* you write that counts.

5 Make sure you sell yourself in all your aspects (that synchronised swimming experience must count for something) but remember that they are, first and foremost, looking for a good all-round teacher.

6 Read the person specification and tailor your form for that particular job in that particular school.

7 Flattery actually works. If you think their website is fab, their grounds stunning and their test results unparallelled, say so. But ...

8 ... Don't overdo it. Nobody likes a creep.

9 Word process the form, unless specifically told to use handwriting.

10 If you're applying to several schools beware the copy and paste trap! I have, in the past, received forms that say how much the applicant wants to work in Anytown Primary School – except that's not the name of my school. That'll be the 'no' pile then.

If you are not selected for interview, it is unlikely the school will offer feedback on your application form, as there are just too many. Get a colleague, college tutor or friendly headteacher to check it for you and offer any advice.

The look round (either pre-interview or during interview)

If you are being shown round in a group there is a fine line between being memorable for your intelligence and enthusiasm and being ruled out for being a know-it-all, too-clever-by-half big mouth. Demonstrate your research during the tour, 'I noticed on your website …' or, 'The last Ofsted report commented on …'. Two or three such comments are plenty. The head, or whoever is your tour guide, will notice. More than a couple of comments and they may well feel it is they who are being interviewed by you – and they may be worried they're not going to get the job. These 'look rounds' really are the first part of a selection process, so treat them with suitable respect and preparation.

Unless you're given name badges (rare), the school might not remember who that incredibly astute and intelligent person was (you, silly). Wear a distinctive tie or top, maybe, but don't take it too far – the school is unlikely to say, 'The one with the pointy hat/revolving bow tie was good!'

brilliant tip

When you visit a school, always talk to the children. Sit next to them at their table, get down on the floor with them and join in their activities. You would be amazed at how many interviewees – out of timidity or disinterest – fail to do this. The host school will be watching and it will make a big difference to the way they perceive you as a potential future colleague.

Talk to the teachers, the admin. officer and the caretaker. It may surprise you, but these last two are often key players in a school and can hold some sway. Apart from anything else, it demonstrates your ability to get on with the team – often high up on the list of desirables in any person specification.

Headteachers will think, 'If you come and visit my school, it gives you a chance to see if you want to work with me in my school and whether I think you might have what it takes to do the job.' Remember, impressions are formed in the first five seconds of meeting: smile.

impressions are formed in the first five seconds of meeting: smile

Talk to staff, talk to children. The headteacher will always ask them what they think. If you are offered the opportunity to wander the school before the interview, take it – don't hide in the waiting area. Find out which members of staff are on the leadership team and chat to them especially – if it's a tight decision, the panel may seek their opinion informally and, if you've stood out for your friendliness without being pushy, it might just swing things your way.

Interviews and presentations

Present yourself smartly. Look like a professional in how you dress. Oh, and don't be orange – fake tans may get you a job in, well, a tanning salon, but I would advise minimal make up for a primary school job. And none if you are a man, sorry if that's sexist, guys. I was once told by an inspector that dirty finger nails have cost more people jobs than anything else so, if you've been pricking out your runner beans that morning, give your nails a good scrub.

If you are given the opportunity to stay in school all day while others are interviewed, take it. It looks more keen than sloping off to the shops/pub/betting shop, and gives you more time to show the school how brilliant you are and how mad they'd be not to appoint you.

If you are asked to do a 10-minute presentation or a 20-minute lesson, make sure it doesn't go over time – finishing early trumps finishing late. Ask the panel to give you a minute-to-go warning, or simply put your watch face up on the table in front of you, and – even if you have not finished – come to your conclusions in good time.

Use PowerPoint to show you can, but don't riddle it with gimmicky sounds and transitions. Don't simply read out what's on the slide. Use a single heading/illustration as a starting point for what you say. If you have prepared well, you might invite questions on aspects of the presentation during it – but stick to the time limits.

If you are asked to teach a lesson, or part of one, you may be given a specific brief (teach a maths mental starter for 30 mixed ability Year 3 children) or an open brief (you will have 30 Year 3 mixed ability children and 30 minutes: do an activity that will show us how you interact with them). There are some dos and don'ts.

brilliant dos and don'ts

Do

✔ Teach to your strengths. If you have a choice and know you are strong on science, teach that. If you know you are pathetically awful at PE, steer clear.

✔ Reinforce positive behaviour. If a child misbehaves, then deal with the situation as you would normally – don't shy away from it because you are being watched. A brief word beforehand to enquire about the school's rewards and sanctions would be helpful. Hint: younger primary school children will do almost anything for a sticker, so maybe dangle those as an incentive at the start of your slot.

✔ Find out in advance if you will have a classroom assistant. If so, involve them as fully as you can – the panel certainly will ask their opinion of you.

✔ Show that you can spot different abilities and adapt your teaching accordingly. A good way to start a lesson with an unknown class is the classic AfL technique of, 'Tell me what you know about ...'. Their answers will allow you to tailor your teaching to their needs and impress the observers no end.

Don't

✗ Go over time – big mistake.

✗ Talk so much that the children never get started on the activity.

✗ Get sidetracked from your intended learning outcomes. You may hear a lovely story of how one child's hamster escaped and hid in the fridge, but probably it is less than relevant to the long division work you had told the panel you were going to do.

✗ Be over-reliant on whizzy technology. Harcombe's First Law of Sod states that, 'If you are desperate for IT equipment to work smoothly, it will not.' I once saw a teacher set up a fantastic IT input to a maths lesson only to flounder because she had prepared it for the wrong model of interactive whiteboard. She didn't flap, thought on her feet and did a great piece of interactive learning, which showed her resilient and flexible personality. She got the job.

✗ Bring to interview your carefully compiled and treasured 'portfolio' of work – photos of you on a school trip, examples of children's work, etc. With five or six interviews/presentations to get through, there simply isn't time and seldom interest.

Questions you may be asked

However the panel phrase questions, they should not be able to throw up anything that you are not prepared for. Questions for class teacher posts will, almost certainly, pertain to the following.

● What makes a good lesson/what have you learned from a poor one?

● How do you encourage good behaviour and manage and correct bad behaviour?

- How do you build good relationships with children/parents/colleagues?
- How would you/your colleagues describe your strengths and weaknesses? (Clearly, refer to four strengths and to one weakness! You can even make the supposed weakness something of a strength – 'I'm a perfectionist' or, 'I keep taking on more work because I love it'.)
- How would you ensure that you met the needs of a wide ability range? (From special needs to average to more able/gifted.)
- How do you plan and assess?
- How do you ensure children are safe and cared for?
- Has there been anything that's caught your eye in the news lately in relation to education?

And that's about it. The questions may be dressed up in different ways or presented as scenarios, but there is not much new under the sun and, if you swot up good answers to these (and are able to identify the questions), there should be nothing to faze you. By 'faze' I mean … that carpet staring moment. You've just been asked a question on assessment and right now you haven't the foggiest idea what to say. In fact, although you wrote an assignment on assessment just a month ago, right at this moment the word might as well be an obscure Lithuanian slang word of which you've never heard. Buy time. It is always OK to say, 'Can we come back to that later, my mind's gone blank.' (Though there are exceptions to this strategy – don't use it if, for example, the panel has just asked your name!)

brilliant tip

Don't be afraid to sound eager – but not desperate. Make it difficult for them to turn you down. If they have a 'Is there anything

you would like to ask or tell us?' moment, take advantage of it,
not to ask a spurious question but to nail your colours to the mast.
'Having looked round the school, I just feel I could make a real
contribution here as well as learn a great deal from the existing
team.' At the very worst the panel might think, 'Creep!', but at best
it might be what persuades them to choose you over someone else
– 'They would both do a good job here, but X has the edge because
she/he really wants to work in our school.'

Remember to make eye contact with all those on the panel –
without looking like you're scanning the room for snipers. Smile
– when appropriate. Lean slightly towards your questioner.
Don't act so relaxed that you're
sprawled on your seat like Cleopatra
on a chaise longue, nor so tense that
you look like the guilty party in a
police interview suite.

> make eye contact with all those on the panel

If your unique selling point includes a sporting, musical,
artistic or linguistic skill – make sure you draw attention
to it without appearing to be a one-trick pony. For most
class teacher appointments, heads are looking for a good all-
rounder. Being able and willing to run an extra curricular
activity, though, is never a hindrance and often a help. You
might volunteer to go on residential trips. Anything that adds
value to your application is useful – providing the bread-and-
butter foundation of being a good all-round class teacher is
in place.

If, in the course of a selection process, even at interview, you feel
this is not the setting for you, then withdraw, quietly and with
dignity. Don't run blubbing from the room. Ask for a quiet word
alone with the head of the panel – usually the head or chair of
governors – and explain how you've decided this is not the right
place for you and you'd like to withdraw.

If asked for questions at the end, a good one is, 'What opportunities will there be for training/development here?' Avoid nitty gritty questions like, 'When is planning, preparation and assessment (PPA) time?'

It is also likely that you will be asked, 'If you are offered the job, will you accept it?' This is standard practice and you need to be ready with a decisive answer. I have heard some people say, 'Erm …', which tends to rule them out of the running anyway.

If you are not successful on this occasion, you may be feeling very low, but always take advantage of any feedback the school offers – ask if you can ring back if you can't face it there and then.

If, as is likely having read this book to prepare, you are offered the job, then enjoy the moment. Make sure you arrange to spend time in the school, even with your soon-to-be new class, before you take up your appointment. Get phone numbers/emails of your new colleagues who will be only to eager to support you and enjoy the time you have to prepare before you get your very own class.

Summary

The professional expectations of you as a teacher are clearly codified – familiarise yourself with them and always try to live up to them.

Being selected for a teaching job is a process that you can understand. Make sure you do everything you can – from application to interview – to make it easy for the selection panel to choose you and, conversely, difficult for them to reject you.

Interviews are seldom life or death experiences, though they may seem it at the time. Prepare, be yourself and try and enjoy it.

If at first you don't succeed, learn from the experience and move on.

CHAPTER 2

Working with colleagues

I n this chapter we learn successful ways of working with headteachers, fellow teachers, teaching assistants and other school staff, and how to overcome common problems.

Having colleagues is a wonderful thing. To work with someone else suits us, because we are gregarious creatures. Humanity achieves its greatest successes through cooperation and collaboration and, as teachers, we succeed partly through working with colleagues who often become our closest friends.

Paradoxically, colleagues are also, potentially, the biggest blocks to you achieving anything and can become your greatest enemies.

There you are in your new school, fresh of face, bright of eye and bushy of tail, walking in to do the job for real for the first time after your interview. You probably will be feeling a mixture of anticipation, excitement and trepidation. There are a few things you need to remember as you walk through the car park to your new place of work.

The first, and possibly most important, thing to remember, is that they want you. You were chosen, deliberately and after earnest discussion, from many others. The interview panel asked you searching questions, almost certainly watched you in the classroom, noted how you interacted with children and colleagues and liked what they saw enough to offer you a contract. They were working to a detailed person specification that you met. Others were rejected in favour of you. You are very much wanted.

I say all this, because you might well be thinking, 'Am I good enough? Can I do this job?' The answer should be a resounding, 'Yes!'. Interview processes are more rigorous than they have ever been and, at the end of that process, you came out on top.

The next thing to remember is that passing the selection process is only the first hurdle. You now have to walk the talk, day in day out, for the remainder of your time at your new school.

brilliant tip

Remember, you were appointed on potential – you are not expected to arrive as the finished article. You will have time to 'grow into' the job.

Bear in mind, also, how your new colleagues will be feeling. Almost certainly, they will be looking forward to your arrival. They will be curious, too. Most of them will have met you only briefly, if at all, at selection and all they will know about you is, maybe, your previous school or training institution.

First impressions count and you need to make sure the first impression they receive is a positive one. This is tricky. You need to be friendly without being too gushing, enthusiastic and eager, without appearing to be like Tigger from 'Winnie the Pooh' – bouncy in rather a wearing way.

> make sure the first impression they receive is a positive one

Some teachers joining a new school make the mistake of disguising insecurities by appearing to know it all, or certainly to know more than their new colleagues. This is a mistake. You need them to help you achieve success and, if you come across as over confident or, worse, arrogant, they will be severely disinclined to help you and may even take a schadenfreude delight in sitting back and watching you make the inevitable mistakes. In short, you need to come across as reasonably modest but competent, eager to learn from them without being over reliant on them, and respectful of what they have already built and achieved in the school, even if, in your heart of hearts, you regard them as out-of-date, stuck-in-the-mud, behind-the-times dinosaurs. As I say, you need them to achieve your goals and achieving your goals becomes much more difficult if you alienate your colleagues. Much better to build alliances.

Working with the headteacher

The headteacher appointed you because he/she saw in you something that he/she really wanted for his/her school. It may be that you are a newly qualified teacher in a school where all the other staff have been since before Noah was a boy and you are the new blood that he/she wants to begin to revitalise the place. Or maybe you are an experienced teacher with particular subject skills that the head especially needs to help improve the school.

I say 'the headteacher appointed you' advisedly. Even if there were governors, teachers, inspectors or pupils on the interview panel, it is, invariably, the head who has the final say. The head has invested trust and hope in you and you need to ensure that you repay that. Always remember that it is the head who writes your next reference. That is a position of considerable power over your future career prospects, as well as the prospects of job satisfaction in your current position.

Your headteacher may be very 'hands on', teaching as often as possible and very much in touch with day-to-day life at the chalk face. Or the head might be a remote figure who is seldom seen except when, bearing clipboard and sharpened pencil, he or she ventures into your classroom to sit in judgement on you. Whichever is the case with your school, don't wait for the head to come to you – go to them and make yourself known. If you have an idea for an improvement to something the school does, take it to the head. Just as you would with any colleague, pop in to do the usual 'good morning' and other pleasantries with the head – some people avoid this from a misplaced sense of not disturbing someone who clearly is too busy or too unapproachable, or not wanting to appear too sycophantic. Believe me, the head will appreciate such niceties just as much as anyone else does.

There is another good reason for forming an alliance or a close working relationship with your headteacher and that lies in tapping into the expertise, skills and experience they have acquired to reach their elevated position.

brilliant dos and don'ts

Do

✔ *Communicate*: headteachers are extremely busy and, as much as they might want to, may not get out to see you in your class as often as you or they would like. So you go to the boss! Pop your head round the office door to say 'hello' in the morning and 'goodbye' at the end of the day. Seek the headteacher out at other times, too (without becoming a stalker, naturally). In busy schools and, given the head's position as boss, not many staff have the time or inclination to look out for the head's welfare – you can be that person. This does not mean you are a creep. It means that occasionally you will ask out of genuine interest, 'How are you?' Basic decency, really, that is often forgotten because of the head's place at the top of a hierarchy.

✔ *Help*: if the headteacher seems stressed or inundated with work. Simply asking, 'Is there anything I can do to help?' will be welcomed by a beleaguered boss. You can make practical offers, too: take assembly, write a newsletter, or any of the other thousands of relatively minor tasks that can relieve the head to do something slightly more pressing.

✔ *Support discussion*: especially at staff meetings. If the headteacher is trying to introduce something new that the existing staff are sceptical about, but you think is a fantastic idea, help the head by supporting the idea with your colleagues in an open way. Without alienating your new colleagues, clearly. (Tricky business this, isn't it?!)

Don't

✘ Join in whinge fests about the headteacher behind his or her back. There are two good reasons for this. The first is that it is unprofessional. If you have a problem with someone, be brave and upfront and have it out with them. Second, the headteacher inevitably will find out.

Working with teaching assistants

Teaching assistants (also variously known as learning support assistants, classroom assistants or special needs assistants) are an enormous boon for most teachers. Working closely with you, they can help transform learning in your class – taking a group while you work with the rest, or vice versa; helping you set up for a lesson; gathering resources for you and a million and one other things. They can be trained by you in your individual way of working and the good ones end up thinking just like you and doing things before you have even asked them to.

brilliant tips

Getting the most from teaching assistants (TAs)

● Communicate with them so they are clear what you want. If you think you are going to forget, write it down in a book which the teaching assistant can check at the start of the next session.

● Don't give them just the low-level stuff. These staff used to be known as 'non-teaching assistants', but now they teach

▶

for virtually all their time. Make use of their skills to take the children's learning forward.

- Don't give them the same group of children every time. This tends to be the children with learning difficulties. This means that you become deskilled in teaching these children and the TA never gets the chance to challenge the more able groups. Ring the changes.

- Value your TA. Give the same sort of praise that you give the children and that you like to receive yourself. If the TA has done something particularly well, say so!

- Train your TA. If there are particular techniques you use, if there are particular questions you want the children to be asked, make sure your TA knows what they are. Be explicit as this often avoids misunderstandings.

Misunderstandings and mismatches of personality can and do occur, however, and they need to be managed sensitively.

brilliant example

When your TA is more of a hindrance than a help

In the first weeks of term, a teacher new to the school was getting to grips with the job really well, benefiting from a highly experienced TA who knew the routines of that class inside out. At first, the TA was really helpful and seemed to enjoy taking the teacher under her wing. The teacher, though, was a little uneasy. The TA kept talking about the previous incumbent in glowing terms: 'Your predecessor used to …' or 'Your predecessor and I always …' or 'Why not try this? I remember when your predecessor …'

The teacher began to feel like the new wife in the Hitchcock thriller, *Rebecca*, constantly kept in the looming shadow of her seemingly perfect predecessor by the mad and sinister housekeeper.

The teacher had already expressed mild concern to a colleague who had said, 'Oh, don't mind her, that's just the way she is with everyone.' This reassured her for a day or two, despite the fact that the TA, when assigned one task, inevitably would drift off to do a different one without so much as a by your leave. Determined not to be overawed by the more experienced and older TA, the teacher always pointed out these instances and the TA seemed genuinely apologetic each time.

Things came to a head when the teacher had rearranged the furniture at the end of the day in readiness for the next morning's activities. She surveyed her work, nodded with the satisfaction of a job well done, closed the door and headed for home, thinking that she had turned the corner as regards her troublesome TA.

The next morning, she arrived with something of a spring in her step which lasted until she opened her classroom door and stood rooted to the spot – all the furniture had been returned to its original configuration. To say a shiver ran down her spine and her blood ran cold might be overstating things, but you get the picture. Was it a poltergeist? A practical joke? Quick checks with the caretaker and the teacher next door revealed, as expected, that the TA was to blame.

Inwardly seething, the teacher sought out the furniture remover and, curbing her natural inclination to unleash furious abuse, questioned her motives. The TA responded that she thought the other way was better and she didn't want the teacher to make a change that wouldn't work and would affect the routine that the children had become used to.

Making sure that they were in a private place, where no one else could overhear, the teacher stated calmly and (given the circumstances) very reasonably, that she was in charge of the class – and its fixtures and fittings – and, whilst she always welcomed advice from the TA and was happy to discuss such things with her, the final decision rested with her and she did not expect to be undermined.

The teacher turned smartly on her heels and strode off having made her feelings very clear. Sensibly she took the precaution of informing her own line manager about what had happened and how she had dealt with it.

What can we learn from this? As I say, it is by no means unusual, though rarely as dramatic as the above example.

First, a problem like this cannot be ignored. The above example actually happened. If you ignore it, rest assured it will not go away. On the contrary, it will get worse until you no longer feel you have any control over your day. Far better to face the problem head on in a polite but firm manner, itemising specifically the things that concern you and setting out, equally clearly, the way you expect things to happen from this point on. Check afterwards that the TA understands precisely what your expectations are. You could, of course, follow up the meeting with a brief written account of what was agreed so that you have a written record for future reference. If you find this sort of conversation difficult – and few of us would find it easy – refer it to a senior colleague or the headteacher, again with clearly itemised instances of what appears to be going wrong.

Second, relationships are dynamic processes that involve two or more people. That is to say, you have a role to play in how good or bad the relationship is. You might well want your TA to lead everything about your professional life. Better though to begin a real professional dialogue where you are the senior partner but always valuing what your TA colleague brings to the table.

Finally, always remember that, whilst working with other people is how you achieve many wonderful and fulfilling things, other people are also the biggest blockers of change. Because you are level-headed, reasonable and consummately professional, do not assume that other people are too.

Working with the support staff

It has been said, by me amongst others, and only half-jokingly, that the two most important people in a school are the school secretary (sometimes called the admin. officer) and the caretaker.

Just watch from the sidelines on a morning when the secretary is absent (though that in itself is a practically unheard of event) and see the near chaos that ensues. Queues of parents with queries about uniform, book bags and dinner money, children looking for minor first aid, the phone ringing continuously and the head and assistant secretary looking harassed and beleaguered.

At this point you are probably thinking, 'That is very admirable – but what, pray, does it have to do with me and being a Brilliant Teacher?' What it has to do with you is that there is little a good secretary does not know about a school and the people in it. She/ he will have excellent powers of organisation and multi-tasking as well as being completely unflappable. In short, she is worth getting to know and worth keeping on the right side of. For the most part, this is just a matter of common courtesy. The usual 'good mornings' and 'byes' but also asking how she is, sympathising when she is snowed under with work and not adding to her workload by messing up your registers, dinner money, trip money or orders for supplies. The good news is that, if you have been kind to her, when you (as you will) mess up one of those things she will be equally kind to you and teach you how to get it right next time. Quite apart from this, school secretaries – or the good ones at any rate – invariably are charming, warm, intelligent, perceptive and fantastic people to know.

> there is little a good secretary does not know about a school and the people in it

The school secretary will also be a font of knowledge about many, if not all, of the families in the school, possibly over several generations, their foibles and peculiarities, knowledge which may be of great assistance to you if you take the trouble to ask her. She, in turn, will appreciate you valuing her opinion. Speaking of foibles and peculiarities, she will also have very good tips on how to handle the headteacher. One such secretary advised a young teacher, 'If you want something from the head, never ask her first thing in the morning: she is not a 'morning person'. Much better to leave it till after lunch.' That is a small piece of advice, but potentially is very valuable to you.

The school secretary also handles things like pay and travel claims, petty cash and the like. If you make her job easier by being kind and considerate and following the procedures she advises, she will bend over backwards to make sure that anything you need is done.

Working with the cleaning and caretaking staff

If your class carpet, which was spotless this morning, is now covered in bits of sticky clay from your art lesson and the sink is blocked from glue and poster paint, do you really want a cleaner/ caretaker whom you haven't been nice to? When your radiator packs up in January or you want to stay at school an hour after the caretaker normally locks up, do you think you will receive unstinting help from someone you have never actually bothered to pass the time of day with?

As with the school secretary, just imagine for a moment what life would be like if a lottery win led to the caretaker's disappearance to Rio de Janeiro. Soiled carpet, blocked sink, you might even have to close your own windows and shut your own computer down at the end of the day rather than leaving it to the poor caretaker.

Caretakers and cleaners are people as worthy of your respect as those of your colleagues who are in much more elevated positions. A caretaker with whom you have dealt at least respectfully and, hopefully, better than that, will let the headteacher know what a nice person and brilliant teacher you are. This might butter few parsnips when it comes to pay increases at performance management time, but it will certainly do more good than harm.

Staff meetings

What are your staff meetings like? Do you look forward to them eagerly because you know professional enlightenment is guaranteed, or do you trudge along to them reluctantly because they are a time-consuming compendium of imprecations to work harder and longer to no greater effect? Do they take place in a business-like atmosphere around a conference table, or slumped in an armchair in the staffroom where the only relief from the headteacher's drone is the inevitable parade of teachers to and from the kettle and biscuit tin? That is to say, are your staff meetings professional forums or ad hoc information overload?

Essentially, staff meetings are what the staff make them – and you, no matter how inexperienced, are part of the staff and have an important role to play.

brilliant tips

- Try not to spend all your time making notes – the likelihood is you will seldom, if ever, refer to them again. Staff meetings should have someone taking minutes (or, at least, brief notes) which will act as an aide-memoire for you.

- Do join in. New and inexperienced teachers have views too and they may well be a breath of fresh air. The likelihood is, if you do not understand what is being said, you are not alone: why not be the one to say, 'Can you run that past me again, but more slowly. And in English.' You will find your colleagues nodding in agreement.

- Try not to be negative. This does not mean that you never question what happens, rather that you do so in a way that aids understanding and doesn't throw a wet blanket of negativity over the proceedings.

- Suggest changes. Why not hold staff meetings in a different classroom every week so each teacher can explain how their

▶

class operates and share any good practice that happens there? Why not have 10 minutes each week devoted purely to sharing tips on teaching reading/number/drawing/whatever?

Staffroom foibles

Your staffroom is the teacher's retreat. In here you will discuss key professional issues over a cup of coffee/tea/organic hedgerow raspberry infusion: what do you think of the Rose Review on the curriculum? Are Ofsted right in saying that schools over-identify special needs? Where did you buy those shoes?

What I am getting at is that the staff room is where the professional and the personal meet, where you can let off steam after a difficult session, share ideas, thrash out planning and, yes, swap fashion tips.

You may be new to teaching, or just new to teaching in this school, but every staffroom is a little different – with rules and rituals all of its own. You need to learn to read these so you can fit in and/or change them to ones you can actually live with.

Some staff see their room as such a refuge from the rigours of teaching that they will have a rule about never 'talking shop' whilst in there – trying to separate work from play. They just want to switch off, relax with a hobnob and recharge the batteries so they can face their next lesson with renewed vigour. Other staff relish the formal and informal professional dialogue that can go on in there. Learning from others, sharing tips and ideas, supporting one another in the daily challenge of being a primary teacher.

brilliant example

You breeze into the staff room on your first morning, grab a cup and set about making a heart-warming, refreshing hot drink. You chat with your colleagues about how the morning has gone thus far and bask in the warmth of a shared endeavour.

Then someone says, 'Has anybody seen my mug?' and the room goes quiet, like the western when the baddie strolls into the saloon bar. You notice, with a feeling of discomfort, that all eyes are on you – and the mug from which you are drinking. 'Oh! Is this yours?' you ask weakly. The staff wait with baited breath and the air is filled with the taunting, tinkling sound of pins dropping as you turn, throw out your barely drunk coffee and wash the mug in the sink before handing it back with many apologies to its one true owner who almost snatches it from you in a decidedly disdainful manner.

The point of relating such a trivial anecdote – one that has been experienced many times by many teachers in many such staffrooms – is because it happens and you need to understand what lies behind it. Some people simply are possessive about drinking vessels. Maybe it is a treasured present from a favourite pupil or a beloved relative. Perhaps it is the finest bone china and a drink will not taste the same in any old cup. Or possibly the owner of the cup is point scoring, making a mark that tells you that uppity newcomers are less than welcome. The teacher in this example took the route of least resistance, deciding it was not worth making a fuss about on her first day. The alternative might have been to say with affected surprise, 'Wow! I'd heard stories about people with their own special mugs but thought that sort of thing went out with chalk and blackboards!'

You choose. The real killer is when you are drinking from another's special mug whilst sitting in another colleague's favourite chair. It happens.

brilliant activity

Things to do with colleagues (and making good use of PPA time)

- *Moderate children's work*: get together at least once every term to mark against national curriculum levels some children's written work in maths or English. You can mark it separately and see if your marks agree, or mark it together, discussing as you go why it merits a particular level and what it needs to reach the next level. This is great professional dialogue and is essential to improve your skill at assessment for learning.

- *Plan together*: with and for each other. If you are in the same year as a colleague this can lighten the load considerably and enable you to plan to your strengths. If you have a scientific bent, you might plan science for both classes whilst your colleague's English degree means that he or she can do some whizzy planning for that. You learn from each other as you do it.

- *Team teach*: share the presentation of a lesson either with one class or both combined. Again, you will learn from each other and not just subject knowledge. Watch how your colleague handles behaviour or questioning and learn some generic teaching skills too.

- *Watch each other teach*: you may freeze every time the headteacher or an inspector comes in to watch you teach. Having a trusted colleague in the room, however, is much less stressful. You can agree a particular focus beforehand – maybe introductions or plenaries – and make sure the feedback includes three positives to every area for improvement. That way the positives make you feel good and the areas for improvement are manageable.

- *Look at data together*: this is especially helpful if one of you finds data baffling. Begin by looking at starting points and compare them to the level the child is meant to reach by the end of the year. Are they on track to make it? If they seem to be falling behind you can share ideas to help them catch up. If they are doing particularly well, try and identify what it is that has helped them succeed and then you can use it for similar pupils.

Colleagues in other schools

Often, schools who feed into the same secondary school (sometimes called clusters or pyramids of schools) have some form of arrangement for their teachers to work together and share expertise.

- You get to learn about practice beyond the confines of your own school: this will lead you to think, 'Wish I worked there!' or 'Thank goodness I don't!'
- You can sometimes borrow resources that your own setting lacks.
- You can share the workload of introducing a new initiative, e.g. a new history curriculum. Much more efficient for five schools to do it together.

Mentors and beyond

If you are a newly qualified teacher (NQT) you will have a mentor (sometimes referred to as an induction tutor) whose role it is to nurture you through your probationary year. This person will be chosen for their experience. Sometimes this means they are a teacher of many years' standing, occasionally it is a highly skilled teacher with only a couple of years' experience, which gives them the advantage of having recent experience of being an NQT themselves.

Whichever it is, they will be an enormous aid to you in many ways. Familiarising you with the routines and ways of working of that school, assisting you with planning, assessment and record keeping and helping you manage the workload (the day in day out, 'Stop the world; I want to get off' nature of your first year is quite unlike anything you will have experienced on teaching practice).

Make the most of your mentor. Try not to worry about being an imposition on them or taking up their time. They will have volunteered for the role in the full knowledge of how time-consuming it is. Above all, do not try to struggle on without their support, giving the appearance of being on top of everything when you may be floundering. This syndrome has been likened to a swan: all above the water is serene, controlled and calm, whilst beneath the water they are paddling away like mad. If you are having a problem, acknowledge it, share it and seek your mentor's help in finding a solution – it is more than likely that your mentor will have spotted your difficulty anyway and will be waiting for you to raise it first, as a good mentor does.

Having a great relationship with your mentor is wonderful, but that should not stop you from forging links with other members of staff too. Your mentor has a specifically designated role and is given time to fulfil it, but there may be others with whom you feel equally, or perhaps more, in tune. They may be nearer your age, more the type of teacher you would like to be, or a specialist in your particular area of interest. The relationship with your mentor should not exclude all others. The more links you forge, connections you make, the wider your experience and expertise will become. More is more.

Other colleagues within school

Subject leaders are a huge untapped resource for class teachers who try to do everything themselves. Stuck for how to make a moving toy for DT? Ask the DT subject leader. Unsure about the difference between a homonym and a synonym? Ask the English coordinator.

The school's SENCO is seldom there to *teach* your children with special educational needs – that is your role: the SENCO will advise you and help you monitor how well, or if at all, an intervention programme is working. This has implications for the way you group children in your class, the idea being that you group together children with similar difficulties because it would be unmanageable for you to provide one-to-one tuition for every child.

The SENCO, as well as being an invaluable source of advice, will also have a range of resources – from pencil grips to word games and software – that will help you implement your planning for SEN problems.

For the brightest or most talented children, there will be a teacher with responsibility for gifted and talented (G&T) – just when you thought G&T was a way to wind down – children. Children on the G&T register may be there for excellence in English or maths, or perhaps for a talent in music or art, or prowess in sport. Whichever it is, the G&T teacher will, like the SENCO, provide you with advice and resources.

If you are an ICT whizz kid yourself, you might not need the services of the school's ICT technician for day-to-day work, but when it comes to blown projector bulbs, recalcitrant printers and the like, you really do not have the time to troubleshoot: use the expertise of the person whose job it is.

To summarise, while your first port of call for assistance will be your mentor or induction tutor, there is a whole crowd of people, with many years of experience, on whom you can and should call when you need help. Don't be shy about it or feel that asking for help is a sign of weakness: it is actually a sign of professionalism and excellent time management and common sense. Remember, 'Shy bairns get nowt'.

Colleagues beyond your school

There are many 'outside agencies' that will support your work as a brilliant teacher. The Educational Welfare Officer is there to help you with children whose attendance or punctuality is poor. Schools have monitoring systems that will pick up persistent absentees but, if you feel concerns aren't being picked up by the school's leadership team, you need to bring it to their attention.

Some schools employ the services of a behaviour support team or consultant. These are called in to deal with particularly challenging behaviour issues and may work one to one with children as well as advising you on strategies to employ in your day-to-day teaching with individual children. Bear in mind that they rely on detailed feedback from you to get the right prescription, so if a strategy is not working they need to know. Remember that there are rarely 'magic bullets' for behaviour problems and some 'solutions' can take many months to take effect.

Many children, particularly younger ones, receive support from speech and language therapists. They will analyse the child's particular needs and set exercises that you, or your teaching assistant, can do with them on a daily basis.

Summary

Be a part of the team and be inclusive about who comprises that team. Politeness and friendliness and showing an interest in others costs little except time and will make your own life easier and more pleasant.

Most of your contact with colleagues will be with those in the same key stage or in parallel classes, but don't forget to make use of the headteacher's expertise too, as well as colleagues in other schools.

In your school staff, there are probably dozens, if not hundreds, of years of teaching experience (OK, so not all of it will be *good* experience). Tap into it by working with lots of different teachers.

Not every colleague will think you are brilliant. This is normal. Don't fret about it and simply get on with doing a brilliant job alongside or in spite of them.

CHAPTER 3

Brilliant
learning

I n this chapter we learn which teaching methods pay off and which don't, the best ways to make use of visits and visitors, and why learning outdoors is so effective.

Conditions for learning

Before a child is ready for learning certain conditions need to be in place. The child needs self-esteem in order to feel capable of learning. Primary teachers are particularly good at building self-esteem in the child by valuing them as an individual, irrespective of whatever talents or academic abilities they may possess. They nurture them through challenges and praise them to the skies when they achieve.

brilliant tip

Names are important. The sooner you are able to address each individual by their correct name, the sooner they will know that you value them as individuals.

A child's home conditions may help them to be ready for learning or they may mitigate against it. A child may come from a warm and loving environment, rich in books and language and characterised by nurture, encouragement and security. Conversely, a child may not be missing just these things, but the adverse conditions at home may even take them into negative territory. If learning is seen as a race – it is not, but bear with the metaphor for a moment – some children would be on the start line, some would be given a head start of 20 metres or so, whilst others would be placed as far behind the starting line as possible. This is the range that primary teachers choose to work with every day, determined that all the children in their care should be helped to reach the finish line. Morally, we cannot concentrate only on the bright and the willing – we must do what is right by all the children we find in our care.

Outdoor learning

One of the best ways to enrich learning and make it memorable and relevant is by getting out of the classroom. Your classroom should be – and probably is – a superbly stimulating, vibrant and exciting learning environment with all the latest resources and gadgets and you, sparkling and dynamic, at its centre. But give the children the chance to get out into a tarmacadamed playground or a green field and they will leap at the chance. Which is as it should be. Children like the comfort of the familiar but they also relish the excitement and difference of the less familiar. They love to explore. Using the space outside the classroom is one of the most important things a teacher can do.

> Using the space outside the classroom is one of the most important things a teacher can do

At a basic level, this could be walking down the corridor to the library, the music room or IT suite. Then you could be out in the school grounds. Even the most spartan of inner city schools have at least a yard, many have much more than that. Or venture out of the gate to the local shops, place of worship, park or other amenity that might be within walking distance. Step on a bus or a coach and go further afield to museums and visitor centres, rivers, theatres, roman ruins and Tudor palaces. Then, instead of returning at the end of the school day, why not stay for several days and do lots of trips and activities to support learning by organising a residential trip. It's exciting me just writing about it.

brilliant example

Ways with outside learning

You can be in a land-locked school, miles from water of any sort, but still learn about how rivers are formed. in your playground with some soil and stones and a watering can or hosepipe.

Make your mountain out of soil and clay, shingle and larger stones. It needs to be only half a metre or so high. Then the rain clouds come – in the form of your watering can/hosepipe and the heavens open. The children can see how the water may form one or more streams as it trickles down from the mountain top and these streams widen as they reach the ground.

This is what used to be called a 'demonstration' lesson and was meant to have gone out of fashion, but I saw it done less than a year ago and the children were absolutely transfixed. Dirt! Stones!! Water!!! All together!!!! They learned in a graphic way what they may have seen demonstrated in a film or on a computer site, but this was in their own playground, so it was much more immediate and captivating. What is more, some of them went home and tried it out there, too. No parents complained, so it must have been alright.

The other factor I neglected to mention was that the teacher demonstrating this did so to 90 children (3 classes) simultaneously which, frankly, only added to the general sense of occasion and my admiration for her chutzpah.

✗ brilliant activity

- *Draw/sketch outside*: simple observational drawing, which can form the basis of more extensive reworkings once you get back indoors. Give them a 'viewer' to help them focus on one particular spot. This is just a rectangle cut into a piece of card, through which the child views the particular part of the scene to be focussed on.

- If you have a bit of greenery, you can give the children the task of finding samples of as many different shades of green as they can – the point of this is not just to observe the rich variety of nature, but also to demonstrate that the tree they always depict as a stick with a green cloud perched aloft is actually a rich cornucopia of hues. Going outside helps the children not just to see but also to observe.

- *Make notes for writing*: writers use notebooks to jot down ideas and observations as they occur to them – why not train children to do the same? Jot down words to describe the clouds or similes to describe the colour of the sky. Write down words or phrases that capture the noise outside. If the leaves in the trees rustle, what do they rustle like? Crumpled paper? The tide on a pebbled shore? Children can keep this book and refer to it for ideas whenever they are called upon to produce a piece of writing.

- *Look for evidence of maths in everyday surroundings*. What shapes are the windows? How many bricks are there in one square metre they chalk on the wall? How long is the playground and how many seconds does it take to run from one end to the other?

- *Take a walk down the high street*: survey the types of shops or offices there. What evidence is there of the printed word? How does this differ from, say, the greengrocers to the solicitors? What evidence of history is there? Do any houses have dates on them? Can we tell their age by the design of their windows and doors?

- *Look at the weather*: how does the temperature outside change from night to day and from season to season. How many hours of sunshine do we get in the autumn term compared to the summer one? How can ICT help us to measure and analyse this information?

● *Place a white sheet under a tree or bush*: give the plant a shake – what sort of things fall onto the sheet? How many legs do they have? Is the body segmented? Do they have wings?

● *Plant some sunflower seeds in different parts of the ground* (shady and sunny): measure their progress over a given length of time. What does this tell you about how these plants grow?

● *Use a camcorder*: record a child running, jumping, skipping, whatever. Play it back through the interactive whiteboard and slow it down. How does the body coordinate? Whilst running, which bit of the foot hits the ground first or leaves it last? What happens to your arms and head when you're running?

● *Teach outside*. Do you always take singing or read stories indoors? Why? There is no finer 20 minutes to be spent than listening to a great story whilst lounging on the grass or seated on a bench under some trees. What better place to sing songs of sunshine than actually in it?

I am sure you can think of lots of ways of using the outdoors in addition to the above list. I haven't even mentioned imaginative play, so important to bring alive subjects like history. That does not mean you give the children swords and shields and get them to recreate a Tudor battle. Although ... Of course, risk assessments need to be made, but these need not be onerous or restricting. It is just a way of demonstrating that the outdoor learning you are planning to undertake is responsible and reasonably safe as well as inspiring and energising.

The weather should be no deterrent, either. If it's raining or a bit breezy, the children will get as much, or more, out of the experience as when it's sunny and still. Providing the children are dressed appropriately (and, if necessary, have a change of clothing with them), there is every reason to get outside to learn on a regular basis.

In short, you should get out more!

If you can't get out, get someone in

Another sure fire way to enliven learning is to invite visitors to your class. Below are just a few suggestions.

- *Parents*: amongst your parents – and this is dependent on the socio-economic make-up of your catchment – you will have people in a variety of jobs and professions. Visitors I have found amongst my parents have included an optometrist, a nurse, a doctor, a builder, a plumber, a trombonist, a soldier, a sailor, a member of a Formula 1 pit-stop crew, a cook, a banker and a digger driver. Their ability to communicate well with the children varies, of course – they are not trained as you are – so you need to structure their visits quite carefully. One way to do this is by devising questions beforehand with the children and giving your speaker some advance notice so they aren't totally stumped for a reply. If it is not related directly to an area of study, it is still relevant because one of the outcomes in Every Child Matters is to prepare children for work (economic well-being). Every Child Matters (ECM) was the government's response to a serious failure of child protection procedures. It aims to ensure five outcomes for all children: be healthy, stay safe, enjoy and achieve, make a positive contribution to the community and achieve economic well-being. You could even get the parent to bring in a 'prop' to help the children guess their occupation. The F1 man brought in a wheel from a racing car!

- *Former pupils*: another rich source – interesting in themselves, but also inspirational by demonstrating what the possibilities are for former and current pupils. I have invited former pupils who are now professional dancers, bricklayers and lawyers.

- *Teachers*: if a teacher has a particular hobby or skill, they can make excellent visitors. Teachers' relatives add to the network. In this area I have had the pleasure of visits from a vicar, a writer and a BBC war correspondent.

- *Pupils*: if pupils have a particular skill, this can be celebrated by encouraging them to talk about it and take a few questions. In this field I have had Irish dancers, stock car racers, athletes, musicians and guinea pig breeders.

- *Visitors from the local community*: nurses, doctors, police officers, firefighters, planning officers (who talked us through how the new shopping centre had been designed), the mayor, the MP and so on.

- Paid visitors: these are really whole school rather than class visitors and cost from about £250 for a few hours. Authors are the most popular and the most easily accessible, often through your local library service. You will also find touring musicians, theatres and storytellers.

If I had £300 to spend and had the choice of 30 text books or an inspirational visitor, I would go for the visitor every time. Costs can be offset by asking for a voluntary contribution of a pound from each pupil in the school, or by asking the PTA to subsidise the cost.

Child-initiated learning

In the early years curriculum it is recommended now that children have a large element of choice in the learning activities they undertake. Why should that stop when they reach the age of five? Why not set aside one session each week, maybe just one hour, when children can pursue their own learning interests? This should not be the woolly 'golden time' or vague topic-type activity, but something with rigour that is assessed and kept on track by the teacher.

It could be working on something that they have found challenging in the past week, or it could be extending the learning they have done in a particular area. The proposed study needs to be discussed briefly with the teacher before it can go ahead and it needs to have real gains in terms of research skills and presentational skills. The finished products will be shared with parents at parents evening and the best will be shared with the whole school at a special assembly.

brilliant tip

As part of a study of Ancient Egypt, the children had to be curators of their own class museum – making and labelling artefacts that the parents then toured. Never have I seen so many mummified Barbie dolls! The learning was memorable and exciting and the parents were delighted.

Offer a choice, also, as to how the work should be recorded – not everything demands lots of writing. Some writing accompanied by photographs and illustrations can be just as powerful as can work that is recorded on video. Some children may choose to offer the finished product as a web page or a PowerPoint presentation.

Children can also shape their own learning in the context of the national curriculum. When you are studying a unit in history or geography, for example, there is some choice in what gets studied in depth and what gets studied in less detail. Why not give this choice to the children? It encourages their independence in learning and ensures that they have a degree of enthusiasm for the work.

brilliant example

A child has been particularly captivated by the study of the Second World War and, in particular, by the story of evacuees. In his one hour personal study time he writes a newsletter to be distributed to all parents and to be placed on the school website asking for stories and personal experiences of evacuation.

The responses are many and include photographs and anecdotes from grandparents.

The child compiles the responses into a booklet, quoting personal reminiscences accompanied by photographs. It is followed up by inviting two of the correspondents into the classroom to be questioned by the children on their experiences. The session is recorded for sound and video and a copy placed in the school library for next year's group to use as a resource. The local newspaper is contacted and runs a short feature on the event.

The child has satisfied a personal interest, created a useful resource for future classes and created genuine links with members of the community.

There are no magic bullets – sometimes it's just hard graft

Since the 1990s, many educationalists and schools have embraced so-called multiple intelligences, as formulated by Howard Gardner, in their teaching and learning. In the mid-1980s, Professor Gardner (a Harvard University Psychologist) put forward his theory of there being more than one type of intelligence. Using this theory to alter pedagogy became increasingly popular in some schools from the 1990s, with some basing their whole curriculum around it. In fact, despite many attempts to do so, no one yet has provided any empirical evidence to support Gardner's theories or shown that they make a discernible difference in practice.

Gardner proposes that there is not just a single intelligence but eight – spatial; linguistic; logical/mathematical; kinaesthetic; musical; interpersonal; intrapersonal and naturalistic. To this has been added existential intelligence and, no doubt, the list will grow. Common sense intelligence tells us that different people have different strengths, but not that intelligence can be neatly compartmentalised in these ways.

The biggest benefit of the multiple intelligences debate, for those of us in primary schools, has not been that it has transformed how we design learning, but rather it has reminded us that all children are different, they develop in different ways and at different rates and we need to value all their skills and attributes. So the child who is a natural footballer is as deserving of our praise as the child who is a natural mathematician, the child who is dexterous and inventive in designing and making things deserves similar accolades to the child who is years ahead of his age in reading or writing.

> all children are different, they develop in different ways and at different rates

Where the multiple intelligences debate has gone awry is where it has been accepted that, 'Ryan can't add up for toffee but he is very creative.' It is good that he is creative. It is right that we value and nurture his creativity but, when he transfers to secondary school or when he transfers to the jobs market, creativity alone (unless it is exceptional creativity) will not stand him in much stead. He will need to be literate and numerate enough to access the secondary curriculum, to be economically active and, at the end of the day, to have a chance in life.

There is no substitute, therefore, for placing at the centre of all we do the single aim of ensuring that every child that leaves us aged 11 has mastered basic skills. Lots more besides, of course, but basic skills are the bottom line we cannot escape from.

Some casual readers may already have thrown down this book in disgust, but try not to judge just yet. I certainly do not advocate a Gradgrindian programme of tedious exercises in writing and number and rote learning. Far from it. But I do nail my colours firmly to the mast in saying, if a child leaves our care unable to write, read and calculate at a level commensurate with their age, then they have, undoubtedly, been let down by us.

The nineties and noughties in primary schools have seen a proliferation of magic bullet solutions to the problem of stalled progress. Children are dehydrated, they need to drink more water. Children like to learn in different ways – appeal to their visual, aural or kinaesthetic learning styles (VAK) and tailor your lessons for them. Electrical connections in their brains need to be fired up constantly so your teaching needs to facilitate this. All of these techniques are based on common sense and the fact that sometimes they are dressed up by their proponents in pseudo-scientific terms to make them sound more authentic or research-based should not detract from their usefulness as part of the teacher's toolkit. *None of them, however, are sufficient on their own to ensure maximum progress and some teachers, attracted by the notion of a magic bullet or quick fix, pursue them to the exclusion of other methods.* The truth is that teaching and learning often involves hard work.

teaching and learning often involves hard work

It is hard to become a concert pianist or a surgeon. It requires many years of study, practice and effort. There are no short cuts to this, though some methods clearly are more effective than others. Likewise, learning to manipulate numbers or to read requires effort in tandem with appropriate tried and tested methods. It can be hard to learn your multiplication numbers to the extent that you can recall these facts instantly, but it needs to be done.

brilliant dos and don'ts

Do

✔ Make the methods of learning as varied and interesting as possible so that they are less of a drudge – sing things, act them out, mime them physically, but learn them.

Don't

✘ Be in thrall to the proliferation of gurus and consultants. Use their ideas only where they definitely have a measurable impact on learning and don't fall for the pseudo-science that sometimes surrounds them.

brilliant tip

Stand up and shake down breaks

There is a group of children in primary schools who find it hard to sit and work at a desk for prolonged periods. Their attention span is short and they are constantly restless. They like to move about and question, investigate and often find it hard to sit still. We call them boys.

Of course, there are times when children have to sit and make a sustained effort at a sedentary task, especially ones that involve writing, but you can break it up for them by judging the mood and having a brief 'shake down'.

Ask the children to stand at their chairs and do some basic on-the-spot exercises: head rolls, arm and leg stretches, moving a finger, then fingers, then hands, then arms – then sit down again. A simple break like this can reenergise them and enable them to refocus on the task in hand. You can do these sessions to music – the funkier the better – and you will find that children welcome the short break and respond positively with increased concentration.

Brain gym – it's great but it isn't science

Brain gym is a series of exercises combining mental agility with physicality as a means of focussing children, sharpening up their mental and physical reflexes and bringing a sense of fun and active learning to the day. Brain gym has some basis in research but is often dressed up in scientific terms and offered as a solution to problems relating to teaching and learning. Brain gym is very big on hydration – because, its supporters argue, blood contains water and a good flow of blood is vital to the brain. Of course, dehydration will hamper learning, but their blood is not going to dry up in the course of your English lesson. Unless you're really dull. In actual fact, brain gym activities are immensely useful in the classroom – useful but not a science. Don't worry about all the guff about synapses, right and left hemisphere activities, increasing the flow of blood to the lungs and brain neuron activity. It is just another – effective – means of limbering up before a lesson and good teachers were doing it long before someone came up with the catchy title.

Learning in short bursts

Children learn best when they have short achievable goals, which are challenging but achievable. If, for example, they are learning how to write a descriptive sentence, several things need to happen. They need to understand what a descriptive sentence is. This may come through teacher questioning – which is also excellent assessment for learning – or it may come from chatting to a partner for one minute and then feeding back to the class. Two or three may be composed from the children's suggestions and the various components identified and exemplified and displayed on a board or on the wall. All of this can be achieved in five minutes. Then the children need to 'have a go' themselves. This could be individually on paper, on a laptop or on a write on/wipe off board. They then share their efforts. Then they talk to a partner about whether what they have come up with actually is a descriptive sentence – has it met the criteria that were displayed in the first five-minute lesson? Can it be improved?

Teacher intervention corrects any misunderstandings and highlights excellent examples for the whole class to see. Then the children are asked to come up with two more sentences, better than their last ones. And that is it. Fifteen minutes max. The objective will have been met – or, if not, the teacher will have identified those that need further practice or help. Job done. Do not flog a dead horse by making them write out 10 or 20 descriptive sentences for the rest of the lesson just to fill time.

brilliant tip

The one, surefire way to improve SATs writing scores is to crack sentence level work. Get that right and pretty much everything else follows.

Pupil talk versus teacher drone

Pupil input is a vital part of learning and brilliant teachers foster and encourage it through regular use, praise and developing a supportive atmosphere in which even the most reluctant speaker feels able to express themselves, knowing they won't be crushed or laughed out of class.

Being given time, space and encouragement to express their thoughts and opinions orally is not just a really good way of learning and of sharing learning but it is a very necessary precursor to becoming skilled at writing in all its forms.

Teacher talk is important to learning too, but there is a lamentable tendency amongst teachers to feel they are truly teaching and earning their salary only if they are talking. This is a mistake. Nothing is more disheartening than seeing a group of children being lectured at by a teacher and spending so much time sitting on the carpet that they are in danger of developing deep vein thrombosis or, at the very least, a numb bum and a frozen brain.

Teacher talk should be brief and to the point. You can be funny, serious, enthusiastic, chiding, encouraging or peremptory but, whichever mode you operate in, for goodness' sake keep it brief. Some teachers fill time with talking because they are ill prepared to teach or because the task they have designed for the children is so fiendishly complicated that it takes several hours of detailed exposition. Remember the acronym of the American Marines: KISS – keep it simple, stupid! Keeping it simple should not mean being simplistic. It is about being clear about what it is you want the children to learn and getting to the nub of the matter without making speeches of Churchillian proportions.

As a rule of thumb, If you are speaking for more than a fifth of the time, you are probably doing too much. That is 12 minutes (or 720 seconds) in every hour, which actually is a devil of a long time. Even adults struggle to concentrate for that long. You may, indeed, be an engaging speaker with something interesting and fascinating to say. But please do not inflict your ramblings on your pupils. Alan Haigh, in *The Art of Teaching* (a book published by Pearson Longman in 2008), suggests that, 'Children … only sit and listen for the number of minutes equivalent to their age. There are bound to be variances but the advice is reasonable.'

brilliant tip

Telling them what it is they are learning is very important. It shows, above all, that you are clear in your own mind what you want them to learn and you are gallantly letting them in on the secret. They then are also able to self- and peer-assess against the criteria you have given them.

Over-learning

This is a technique that does what it says on the tin – you learn something over and over until you have grasped it. Spelling is often taught in this way and also it is used often in number, but can be applied equally successfully to anything you have to learn. It is not as tedious as it sounds and can be done simply by having several mid-session plenaries to remind the children of what they have already learned.

---

brilliant example

In an hour-long lesson, you might check after the first minute, 'What were the names of Henry VIII's six wives?' Some children might know already. Get all the children to repeat the names out loud in unison. Fifteen minutes later, when you are checking on their recall of something else you will ask again, '... and what were the names of Henry VIII's six wives?' More children will be able to rattle off the names now and, again, you get the whole class to do so in unison.

After 30 minutes you check on 2 other things you want them to retain and then ask the six wives question again. Almost all of the children will have recalled them by now. Forty-five minutes in and you will check on three facts you want them to recall and then the six wives. Everyone will have it by now, but you will still revisit it at the end of the lesson.

Then, after afternoon registration, you will ask again. And the next day. The children will see it as a game and they will all be able to rattle them off and be proud of the fact. It is a memory technique that they can apply to anything that has to be learned by heart – not just Henry's missus, but maths rules, science facts, anything!

Listen, see or do? All three, actually

The old adage, 'I hear – I forget. I see – I remember. I do – I understand,' has some useful resonance for teachers, but is not universally true. It harks back to our friend VAK learning and we have already acknowledged that a combination of all three methods is used by brilliant teachers. Clearly, if we are told about something, we will recall it or not based on our level of interest. If we see it, because visual memories are stronger than auditory ones, we are more likely to recall it. If we take part in it so that we can feel, physically and emotionally, what it is like, we may well understand it and certainly find it more memorable. This used to be known as concrete learning and is now referred to as active or hands on learning. See the brilliant example of the river formation lesson earlier in this chapter.

Don't pretend to know everything

Do learning *with* the children rather than *to* them. The children need to see you as a learner too. You may be further along the road than them but you should not set yourself up as some omniscient being who is the source of all knowledge and wisdom in the class. It can be tremendously empowering for the children to hear you say, in response to a question of theirs, 'I don't know – how can we find out?' This kicks in all sorts of positives. They have a sense of working alongside you and helping you, just as you help them. It seems somehow more adventurous and exciting and it allows them to make use of their current research and learning skills and to develop some more along the way.

Summary

Trust what you know works well. Try possible improvements, but don't stick slavishly to any one system – mix and match the best that the education world has to offer: your children deserve it. Beware, in particular, any consultant who claims to have a quick fix or miracle cure. They are seldom quick, they rarely fix and they are never miraculous.

Use the classroom well, but also make use of the outside areas for learning – from the playground, to the locality, to places of interest further afield. Tap into the expertise of parents and others in the community who all have useful and interesting lessons – if you help structure them – to pass on to the children.

Help create the supportive conditions necessary for learning to take place and include the children in designing their own learning and pursuing their interests within the overarching framework of the national curriculum.

Keep your own talk to a sensible minimum and let the children express their thoughts and opinions in speech as often as possible and certainly more often than they have to express them in writing. Recognise that a physical break in the course of a lesson is a good way to break up the learning into manageable chunks and it will reenergise both you and your pupils.

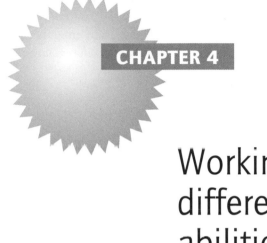

CHAPTER 4

Working with different abilities

I n this chapter we learn how to use differentiation and dialogic
learning to get the best out of the least able, the more able
and the magnificent middle, and we find out why basketball
is better than ping pong.

Introduction

The children in your class may be aged, say, 10 but their ability
age may range from 7 to 13. Each one of them needs to progress
– from where they are, not from where you might like them to
be. This is not an easy thing to achieve, but it is one of the key
moral purposes of education that *every child matters* – not just
the bright, cheerful, successful and hard-working ones, but the
puzzled, bad-tempered, lazy and struggling ones. As a brilliant
teacher, you will want to enrich and stretch the most able, work
to get the average above average and make sure that the below-
average children catch up. Because if you don't, who will?

Children are skilled and astute observers of the world around
them and their own place in it. Ask young children in the
Foundation Stage, and most of them can point out easily who
can already read well, who can draw and colour in neatly, who
struggles with counting, who can run fast, who can't spell their
key words yet, who prefers to work quietly by themselves and
who likes to role play in the home area. Throughout their time
in school, children are very aware of their own diversity – their

differences related to learning ability, cultural background, interests, gender and talents.

No two children are alike and no two children learn at the same rate or in exactly the same way. In class, one of our major tasks is to teach children to think for themselves by giving them the tools and encouragement to do so.

> one of our major tasks is to teach children to think for themselves

While we, as teachers, have long known and attempted to manage this diversity, our response has not always been effective. At worst, we tend to ignore student differences and rely on the 'teach-to-the-middle' approach, where every child has to read the same book, do the same activity, work at the same pace, do the same homework and take the same test.

Frustration on the part of many pupils is the inevitable outcome – those who find the work to be 'easy' and therefore boring, others who find the work too challenging and beyond them, and those whose particular strengths are not addressed. Teachers get frustrated too, because they are not getting the best from every pupil. In trying to provide genuinely challenging and interesting learning for their pupils, many teachers have discovered that they can better meet the diverse needs of the children in their class by differentiating between them by the tasks they provide.

brilliant tip

For the more able, rather than differentiate vertically and take children into the next Key Stage curriculum, enrich horizontally and add depth and breadth to their current learning.

At heart, the aim of differentiating tasks is to maximise each pupil's progress. It should be done by:

- assessing where each pupil is;
- deciding where they need to be;
- closing the gap between the two in the way most likely to succeed for that individual or group.

In practice, it means offering three or four different learning experiences in response to pupils' varied needs.

brilliant tip

Tasks and resources may be varied by difficulty to challenge pupils at different ability levels, by topic in response to pupils' interests and by pupils' preferred ways of learning or expressing themselves, or recording the outcomes.

brilliant tip

Systematic assessment followed by oral and/or written feedback make more difference to a child's progress than anything else. AfL is king.

Gifted and talented (G&T) children – a date with destiny

As you survey your new class, you might well be thinking, 'Gifted? Talented? Where?!' But amongst your 30 apparently ordinary little angels, you do have children who are more able in one or more ways. These are human beings you have in your care and tutelage. This is the same species that produced Newton, Shakespeare, Mozart, Picasso, Gates and Beckham. They all went to school. They all had teachers. Some of their teachers will have identified and nurtured their gifts and talents and helped shape their particular genius. Is that not a thrilling prospect?

Even if you don't have a bona fide genius sitting in front of you, struggling to make sense of fractions or adjectives, you do have children who will go on to be doctors, lawyers, scientists, entrepreneurs and, undoubtedly, teachers. It will be you, dear teacher, who plays a determining role in whether, or at least how quickly, they achieve their destiny.

First, identify them. Your school may already keep a register of G&T pupils, in which case, you will have been alerted on taking control of your class which children have been so identified.

brilliant tip

Familiarise yourself with the Quality Standards for Gifted and Talented (to be found on www.nationalstrategies.standards.dcsf. gov.uk/node/97563) which offers a straightforward means of matching children to criteria.

Don't make it an elitist group or you're setting them up for a fall. Often, by working alongside average or less able peers, G&T children develop their social skills and extend their own knowledge by helping someone else to gain understanding and build up their own self-esteem. The theory is that, by raising expectations for more able children, expectation and achievement will rise for the whole class (known as the 'rising tide' phenomenon; an hypothesis borne out by research). It is important, for example, that children are not always taught in ability sets because the middle ability children then miss out on the role model of the higher ability children. So top-quality G&T provision, far from being elitist, can benefit everyone.

brilliant case study

It has been made statutory since September 2010 that parents should be informed if their child has been identified as G&T and placed on the register. This is fraught with problems. First, sometimes children are identified incorrectly, just as they are for SEN, though the Quality Standards should help here. Second, sometimes children's progress does not follow the trajectory initially indicated.

One school identified a child as more able in mathematics and notified his parents who were, justifiably, thrilled. They had meetings with the teacher and the gifted and talented coordinator to discuss how his learning would be enriched and developed through tailormade programmes. Eighteen months later, despite having the same teacher, his progress had slowed down to something just above average. Those parents then had to be told their son was no longer on the G&T register and, by implication, no longer more able. They were not happy with the situation, again understandably. But children can and do move on and off the G&T register, just as they do with the SEN register.

Parental support and family life will have accelerated the progress of some children early on so they appear to be G&T but this will even itself out after several years of schooling. Progress is rarely a uniform trajectory.

Children's learning will plateau from time to time. It is useful, therefore, when initially meeting with these parents, to say, 'Your child is currently identified as gifted/talented and I will be doing everything to ensure the progress made is commensurate with ability and potential, but children can and do vary in their rate of progress, so don't be surprised or disappointed if your child is taken off the register, possibly temporarily, in future years.' Being open and honest upfront avoids problems later on.

---

brilliant tip

A good way of spotting the bored underachievers is through dialogue and questioning. The articulacy and detail of their response usually will be far in advance of what they might offer through written work.

---

brilliant dos and don'ts

Do

✔ Differentiate homework. Parents who know their stuff dislike homework that isn't differentiated – if you wouldn't do it in a lesson, you shouldn't do it for homework either.

✔ Plan for the most able and differentiate down. This is more likely to ensure expectations are sufficiently high than using the average or less able as your starting points.

Don't

✘ Think that, because the children are set by ability, you don't have to differentiate for them. You will still have quite a wide range of abilities in there. If you don't differentiate within sets you are perpetuating the belief that sets are more for teachers' benefit than for pupils'.

Special educational needs

Depending on your setting, this group could be from 0 to 100 per cent of your class. They may include:

● children with language difficulties: speech problems, dyslexia or general learning delay for example;

● children with autism or aspergers;

● children needing occupational therapy, physiotherapy, parent support advisers or specialist teacher advisors;

● children with behavioural issues (ADHD), etc.;

● medical conditions, such as diabetes, asthma and epilepsy, will all have an impact on activities you provide for such children.

In all of the above cases, while it is primarily *your* responsibility to teach the children, you should be guided and supported by the SENCO and possibly outside agencies, such as educational psychologists and speech and language therapy. You are not expected to become an expert over night, but you will develop your own expertise and areas of interest. Where parents are on board children always do better than those whose parents are not.

Like the gifted and talented group, their needs may vary enormously and it is your task to manage these needs in a planned way. If you are in an Early Years or KS1 class, some of the children identified as having SEN simply might be the younger or less mature ones in your class. It used to be the case that children identified as SEN ceased to be so as they matured and caught up with their peers. Nonetheless, some of their special needs may persist, even though they may decline in severity. Like all children, the key to managing their progress is good use of formative assessment and meaningful individual targets.

brilliant tips

- When using an intervention or 'catch-up' programme, make sure you assess before and after intervention to judge whether it has worked. Not every intervention will work with every child and, if it's not working, you're wasting precious time, effort and resources.

- In planning, be explicit about how SEN children are going to be supported. When you come to review planning you can assess whether the support was successful and, if not, why not. Don't do the same thing week in week out if it is not working.

- IEPs (individual education plans) should be brief, targeted entirely on the specific areas of need and should be working documents that are regularly updated, amended and generally scribbled on.

- Targets need to be short-term, reviewed frequently and updated.

- Success criteria need to be measurable.

Differentiation

Differentiation is not just about task design (what the children are asked to do – easier work for the less able and challenging work for the more able). It is about how the classroom is set up, how children are grouped, how they are questioned and making best use of effective assessment for learning. It is about keeping lots of plates spinning and making sure none crash to the floor.

Most of the time you will differentiate three ways – tops, middles and bottoms – manageable in terms of planning and sufficiently challenging for each of those groups. Less frequently, you will need to differentiate four ways – most able, more able average, less able average, least able. Beware the tendency to miss out the magnificent middle and concentrate on most or least able. Giving the magnificent middle a chance to spark off the more able can often yield fantastic results and raises their aspirations.

More able children will respond better to less structured tasks, i.e. ones where they can decide on the processes themselves. Middle ability can be given a range of structures from which to select. Less able will need more prescriptive structure, i.e. do this followed by this.

So, for example, if you want the children to learn about Forces, less able might be directed to a particular book or website to complete a matrix showing examples of one force, e.g. gravity. Middles might complete a matrix for examples of three forces, say magnetism, gravity and friction. Whilst more able might be offered a range of books and websites and asked to give an overview of forces in general with a detailed look at one. Less able will need texts that they are can read independently, middles need more challenging texts whilst more able will choose their own. How they record their findings might vary: annotate a given picture, make a presentation, record a video design a web page or, simply, write.

You may also differentiate by *time* spent on study. More able will often want to whizz through, but should be given opportunities to study at length and in depth when they have a particular interest. This develops study skills and deepens knowledge. Middles will benefit from not being hurried and will, too, relish the chance to study things in depth.

The range of learning from concrete to abstract is another means of differentiation. At its most obvious this is a matter of the less able using physical apparatus (multilink, number lines, number squares) for calculation, whilst middles might use blank number lines and more able might draw on number facts they had committed to memory.

With less able, challenges will usually (though not exclusively) relate to delay in the skills of reading and writing. In reading they will need a structured programme of phonics plus regular and frequent opportunities to read aloud to a trained adult (and to follow a text that is being read to them). In writing, sentence level work is the key to success, aided by opportunities to talk, prompted and developed by astute questioning, and reading their own writing aloud to a skilled listener. To avoid the child becoming demoralised, the brilliant teacher will offer different ways of recording outcomes as alternatives to the perceived drudgery of writing: sound or video recording, photographic or drawing recording. At all times encouragement and building the child's self-esteem are paramount. A child who feels incapable and unsupported will never progress.

> encouragement and building the child's self-esteem are paramount

Quite simply, differentiation is a range of strategies to manage the ability range in your class and remain (relatively) sane. All children are different. Some need longer to reflect on ideas before beginning to apply them, while others want to get on straight away. Some need to talk as they learn, while others need peace and quiet. Some develop a narrative of their learning to get it clear in their own minds, others make mind maps, and still others might learn and think best whilst manipulating 3-D materials like plasticine.

Interest-based differentiation allows pupils to self-direct their learning along lines they enjoy. For example, in studying the Second World War, one might opt to write a short story about the life of a child during the war. Another might choose to apply key ideas about the war to an investigation of what we regard as heroism then and now. Yet another might prefer to study ways in which the war affected the development of technology.

Flexible grouping should be applied discerningly. In a differentiated class, pupils work in many different formations: sometimes individually, sometimes collaborating in pairs or groups. (Bear in mind, also, that not all group work involves cooperation or collaboration – you can work individually while part of a group.) Sometimes tasks are ability-based, sometimes interest-based, sometimes constructed to match a favoured learning style and sometimes a combination of ability, interest and learning style. In a differentiated classroom, whole-group instruction often is used for introducing new ideas (though questions and prompts will be matched to individuals), for planning and for sharing learning outcomes.

brilliant tip

Children of all abilities will benefit from the use of technology. Not just computers and the internet, but voice recorders and camcorders as a means of recording their work. Put the pens and pencils away for a while!

Pupils almost always learn better when they learn actively and all children enjoy exploration. Teachers guide them and the level of guidance will vary according to task and ability. Because varied activities can take place simultaneously in a differentiated classroom, the teacher works more as a facilitator of learning than as a font of knowledge or a dispenser of information. (But note that the number and nature of activities should not impact on good order and an atmosphere conducive to learning: the 'carousel' of activities can easily turn into a 'circus' if it is not planned and executed with skill.) A key objective of all we do is that pupils must learn to be responsible for their own work. Independence in learning – learning to learn – is always our over-riding goal. Effective target setting and formative assessment through oral and written feedback will accelerate progress towards independence.

> pupils must learn to be responsible for their own work

There are always resource implications in differentiation. The three main routes to differentiation are outcome, support and task.

1 *Differentiation by outcome*: most likely to be seen in language work, especially writing. So, you could set one task for the whole group – writing a persuasive letter, say – and the children would find their own level of challenge. Differentiation by outcome basically is an open-ended task, one in which the children can find their own level.

2 *Differentiation by support*: usually in the form of a classroom assistant or other adult, it is appropriate in all cases, but most often used with SEN. I believe it should also be used regularly to support G&T too. It is important that the support is not always provided by a TA: the teacher should timetable him/herself to work with those children too, to ensure they are getting the benefit of a qualified professional as well as for purposes of assessment and simply knowing your group.

brilliant tip

Avoid over reliance on adult support. Children need to be supported only in order to become independent. Even if parents demand one-to-one sessions it is often more beneficial to support from a suitable distance and put the child in some control of their own learning.

3 *Differentiation by task*: planning intensive (workload warning! you may have to design four differentiated tasks for one single lesson) and most often used in mathematics and information retrieval when studying a text. So more able children will have tasks to stretch their ability to use inference and deduction while the least able will retrieve mainly factual responses with some steps towards simple inference and deduction. Because of the implications for teacher workload involved in differentiating by task, it should not be used for every lesson. That would be unmanageable.

brilliant tip

Strategies such as Philosophy 4 Children work with all abilities to develop questioning and thinking skills as well as improving speaking and listening. Philosophy 4 Children as a system is simply a means of challenging children to consider 'abstract' problems in order to enrich their learning and help develop their ability to think around a given problem. One such starting point might be, 'Why did Little Red Riding Hood wear red?' The range of possible answers really stimulates the children to use their brains.

Apart from these three methods, there are structural strategies that help to differentiate.

● *Differentiating through questioning*: in a rapid-fire mental maths session you need to involve the whole class, but have to vary your questioning to engage all ability levels and to ensure no one feels excluded. One way of quickly assessing the mental maths ability of a new group is by using wipe on wipe off boards (WOWO) and markers. In response to a question, the children write down their answer and hold it up for you to see, enabling you to assess those who are struggling at one end and those who are not sufficiently challenged at the other.

brilliant tip

Questioning and Bloom's taxonomy

Bloom's taxonomy – a ranking of types of questioning – is a useful guide. It divides questioning into knowledge-based ('What happened after ...?', 'Make a list of the main events in ...'), comprehension-based ('Who was the key character ...?', 'Retell the story in your own words ...'), application ('What questions would you ask of ...?', 'Make a puzzle game using the ideas from ...'), analysis ('What were the motives behind ... 'Construct a graph to show ...'), synthesis ('How many ways can you ...?', 'Create a new product and a marketing plan') and evaluation ('Is there a better solution to ...?', 'Make a booklet about five important rules ..., Convince others').

● *Differentiate by teaching more visually*: for example, some children (and not only the less able) might still need physical clocks when doing time in Year 6.

● *Self-differentiation*: requires teacher guidance but is principally founded on children choosing their own entry level to a particular activity. It helps foster independence when children are enabled to choose their own entry level.

- *Using a variety of groups*: self-selecting, by ability, by friendship or association is the norm in many classrooms. Children usually know where they are in the academic pecking order. It is important, however, to ensure that such groupings are fluid, that the middle ability children get the chance to work with the more able (to give them something to aspire to and be challenged) and that children placed in a lower-ability group don't stay there because of the possible self-fulfilling prophecy of low expectations. Likewise, is it right that a child with a real facility for history should be placed in the bottom group because they struggle with writing? There are other ways they can record their work, including the use of voice recorders and camcorders.

brilliant tip

Use able children as 'envoys' – where they work with you and then they reproduce that work with others. This demonstrates their understanding and they may be able to explain it to their peers. Children see this as a real feather in their cap, it boosts self-esteem and is a big incentive for them.

Working with the high flyers – finding texts that challenge and excite

All children should be given the chance to engage with the great classics of literature, sometimes unexpurgated and unmediated, sometimes adapted to hook them. Some teachers will, for example, tell the story of Shakespeare's *Macbeth* to a class or group: it is a gripping tale with lots of twists and turns, after all, and that element will appeal to all abilities. Add to that a few excerpts of Shakespeare's verse – the witches' chants, a Macbeth soliloquy – and it's a safe bet that one or two children will be sufficiently interested to want to read the original play. Some of the descriptive passages in Dickens – the opening to *Great Expectations*, the description of fog in *Bleak House* – also lend themselves to reading aloud. Compare them to filmed versions, being always mindful that films are certified and you should show nothing above a PG, and even that will need written parental permission.

✦ **brilliant** tip

Use Assessing Pupil Progress (APP) materials to work with children at the cusp of levels as it helps identify very clearly the next steps they need to take to close the learning gap. APP materials were introduced in 2008 and help teachers map the incremental stages in a child's learning in reading, writing or mathematics. They are very useful to support the child and the teacher and are widely used as a good assessment for learning tool.

↗ **brilliant** case study

Jabberwocky

Jigsaw groups are a good way of encouraging cooperation (working together on the 'big picture') and collaboration (completing a task as a team). The idea is that three or four groups (parts of the jigsaw) are set, or choose, tasks that, when brought together at the end, reveal the whole picture.

A teacher wanted to investigate learning from a classic poem and chose Lewis Carroll's 'Jabberwocky'. One group had to find out biographical details of the poet using the internet, another had to learn to say the verse aloud with expression, a third group had to devise music to accompany the reading and record how the instruments should be played, while a fourth group had to turn the story of the poem into a series of news reports spoken to camera in the style of television news.   ▶

This last group watched news reports on the BBC iPlayer to learn key features of language used in such reports. The group doing the music had to decide which instruments were most appropriate to accompany different sections of the poem – the relaxed and sunny opening, heightened tension, the battle and the victory – and record their use in a matrix. The group doing the choral speaking took two stanzas each and were coached by the classroom assistant with the aid of a voice recorder so they could critically evaluate their own efforts. The group doing the biographical research had to produce text that could be read aloud in no more than two minutes and find accompanying photographs for a multimedia presentation.

The children worked in self-chosen mixed-ability groups and the results of their work culminated in a performance – biography, poem with music, news report – to parents and the whole school at assembly.

brilliant tips

- One of the best ways to test whether knowledge and skills have been absorbed is to ask children to apply the known into unknown situations, e.g. you know what an adverb is, can you apply its use not just to story writing but also to writing in history, geography and RE?

- Teacher intervention in play can be a key differentiating factor. The teacher's intervention should be what extends the children's thinking by posing a question (which may also be a suggestion) and enabling children to extend the learning they are gaining from the play activity.

Dialogic teaching

Using speaking and listening is not 'second best' to writing. It is a key skill that informs learning. Robin Alexander, in his 'Cambridge Primary Review' (an independent enquiry into the condition and future of primary education in England), talks of the primacy of speaking and listening in developing learning in class: teaching which is 'dialogic' – where classrooms are full of debate and discussion that is 'collective, reciprocal, supportive, cumulative, critical and purposeful' leads to learning that is dynamic and rapid; don't shy away from disagreement and disputational discussions – that is when ideas are honed and articulacy developed; cosy circle time is necessary – on a few occasions – but robust discussion in which all children are supported to contribute is a brilliant team builder, appropriate to all abilities and an exceptionally valuable skill for learning and life.

In developing dialogue, you should avoid the 'ping-pong' model, where the teacher talks, then the child, then the teacher, then the child, and so on. Instead, develop the 'basketball model' where the teacher might start off but then the dialogue goes from child to child without the teacher intervening. This is high-level teaching – keeping your oar out unless absolutely necessary.

Summary

Working with different abilities is one of the most crucial things the brilliant teacher does – it is also one of the most challenging. The bad news is that it can take time to learn how to do it; the good news is that, once you have the knack, you never lose it.

Never teach a child something she or he already knows. Always assess carefully – and assessments don't have to be written and formal – and plan to take them on from where they are. That is the true meaning of personalised learning.

In order to manage the challenge of providing differentiated work you need to develop a range of strategies both in developing a class ethos and in making assessment and self- and peer-assessment central to your work. If children acquire the skills of self-assessment they are well on the way to becoming independent learners.

When you set by ability you will still need to differentiate within a large set. This usually is done across a year group. Ability groups, not requiring internal differentiation, are within your own class.

Remember that children will learn some things in a single 'hit', while at other times they will need to over learn (repeated learning of the same skill) in order to be able to retain and apply.

CHAPTER 5

Achieving brilliant behaviour

In this chapter we learn how to prepare for a new class, the importance of smiling, positive rewards and sanctions.

Remember the first day in a new class? Blinking back anxious tears, the lump in the throat, the trembling lower lip? And that's just the teacher ...

You and your class are going to have a relationship that will last far longer than the one year you are in close day-to-day contact. How you work with them, how you treat them and how they treat you is something that, in many cases, will stay with them for the rest of their lives. Witness the emails, cards and letters that former pupils send to a well-loved past teacher, the happy chance encounters in the street years after they have left your care.

This chapter suggests ways to get the relationship off to a brilliant start and how to maintain and develop it in the course of the academic year so that it is a happy and purposeful time for both you and the children. Key to this is establishing from the outset your expectations of the children's behaviour.

> establish from the outset your expectations of the children's behaviour

Before you become their teacher

Before you get your new class for real, hopefully you will have had
them for one or more induction sessions, where you will have had a
chance to set the tone for everything that follows. If they are a single
class transferring as a unit from one year group to the next, already
they will have quite distinctive behaviour patterns – for better or
for worse – as set by their previous teacher. Many of them will have
grown very fond of your predecessor and will be wary of what they
are going to find in you that will be as wonderful as the relationship
they enjoyed last year. You may hear comments such as, 'Miss X
used to let us …', or even, 'Mr X never used to do that.' You have
to accept this as part of the package of being new to them. If you
have been in the school for a year or so your reputation already will
have gone before you. If you are brand new, as it were, the children
will be wondering exactly what to expect – and they will try and see
exactly what you will allow and what you will not.

In the summer term most schools will have at least one induction session where children get to spend a lesson, a half day or
a whole day with their new teacher. What should the brilliant
primary teacher do to get things off to a great start?

Get to know your children before you meet them

Speak to their current teacher and classroom assistant. Go
through them name by name on the class list. This is sometimes done as a paper exercise with maybe a short face-to-face
dialogue with your colleagues. The face-to-face bit is, in my
opinion, more important than the handover of records, notes
and data. You need to find out who is friends with whom, as well
as which groupings are likely to create an unpleasantly explosive
mix. Which children are on the special needs register, which
identified as gifted and talented? Who are the budding sports
stars, musicians, actors and artists? Are there any medical issues
you need to know about? Are there any child protection issues?

If your school is particularly forward looking, even before transition day you will have a chance to spend a session in class with the children and their current teacher to watch how he/she handles them and to note the group dynamics. Who settles quickly, who distracts themselves and others, who is needy, who is independent, who craves constant attention and who avoids attention at all costs in order to avoid having a teacher keep tabs on him/her?

brilliant example

The children get into pairs. One child has to tell the other all about themselves – in no more than two minutes. The listening child then has to summarise the already potted biography and the subject can give a thumbs up if they have done it particularly well. You can listen in on these conversations and begin to note things mentally like favourite sports teams, books, foods and the like. You could even model the process first by partnering up with an amenable, articulate child whom you will have identified already through your meetings with their existing teacher. The children, of course, will love to hear all about you.

On transition days there are several activities that will help the getting-to-know-you process go smoothly.

brilliant activity

- *Make a passport*: this should include the usual factual details – date and place of birth – but why not add hair and eye colour, height and (more sensitively) weight, shoe size, etc., all of which can be number crunched on a computer to produce graphs and charts for display that can then be updated as the year progresses. The passport can be used later to collect stamps from you for good work or improved effort.

▶

- *Create a display*: this is a good activity as they will then begin to feel the room is 'their' place. This could be a class charter – not just rules for behaviour, but ways in which the teacher and children will collaborate and cooperate to make it a great learning environment for all.

- *Create an ambition tree*: this is another 'getting to know each other' display – it can be a real tree branch (spray it gold or silver if you feel the need) with dangly cards, or a 2D tree on the wall. It should include hopes and aspirations for the future and what learning they will need to do to realise their ambitions. For example, if Scott wants to be a footballer, he will need to learn about fitness and body science. And he can't ignore writing, as he will need this to write his best-selling autobiography for his fans.

- *Design your ideal classroom layout*: again, this gives the incoming children some sense of ownership. This can be done simply by drawing, using plasticine or play dough modelling, or mathematically on grid paper. Of course, the plans can then be turned into reality. It may be that you have several layouts to be used for different sessions and the children have to be trained furniture removers so they can transform the layout in a minute. (Find a piece of music you can play as they do it – just watch them try to finish before the music stops!)

- *Do a circle time activity*: this could be about 'What my friends would say about me', where each child comes out with one such statement. It is actually helpful if the teacher takes part as well – the teacher can model the process and the children will delight in finding out (appropriate) details about you.

- *Play a ball game*: children sit in a circle and roll a ball to someone as they call out that person's name. The teacher joins in and makes sure everyone gets a turn. A great non-threatening way to introduce each other and learn names.

The first term

In the first few days of a new class, set aside some time for one-to-one conferencing with the children. This is about getting to know them as individuals – the better to understand how they learn – and gaining an insight into the 30 different personalities you have in your care.

By the time the children arrive for their first day with you, already you will be well-briefed and you will have begun to acquaint yourself with the 30 personalities whose education is in your hands for the next 10 months or so. The moment finally will arrive when you will be welcoming them into your class for the first time and this welcome is crucially important. Stand near the door as they come in so you can smile and welcome them with warm words, perhaps saying hello to individuals whose names you have already picked up. This also gives you a chance to keep them in order, tell them where they might sit and ensure that the crucial first few minutes establish you as approachable and warm, but very definitely in charge. As you take the register you can say hello to each individual and establish how you want them to respond.

brilliant tip

Should you smile before Christmas?

From the word go it is important that you are clear about your expectations in terms of behaviour. The old adage, 'Don't smile at them till Christmas!' is actually ill advised but has a kernel of truth in the sense that those first few weeks will set the pattern for the rest of the year. If you establish clear routines and procedures in the first few hours and days, it is much easier than trying to retrieve order later on. This may seem a tedious process to an eager new teacher but it is absolutely vital. If you want silence for a good reason then you need to stop them and remind them whenever they stray from your expectation and get too noisy. Initially, this might mean you stopping them seemingly every minute – hence the acknowledgement that the process may appear tedious – but

▶

it is essential that you are clear and consistent. Lack of clarity and consistency will seem very unfair to the children and you will have your work cut out if you don't say what you mean and mean what you say. This does not mean you have to be a nagging misery-guts. Positive reinforcement should be used in a ratio of at least four to one negative sanction.

brilliant tip

The first rule of behaviour management

… is plan and deliver interesting, engaging and (more than occasionally) downright exciting lessons. I have no doubt whatsoever that 90 per cent of poor behaviour starts with lessons that are dull or poorly matched to ability. When the children are actively engaged in their learning they will not think of misbehaving: their attention will be on learning because you have made it so interesting.

brilliant tip

The ancient advice, 'Do unto others as you would have them do unto you,' holds especially true in close-knit places like the classroom. If you want respect from your pupils, you must first give it. If you want them to speak nicely to each other and treat each other well, you have to model that yourself every hour of every day you are with them. Remember that, while you have expectations of them, they have every right to have expectations of you, which also may be enshrined in a class charter to be displayed on the walls. How you will be fair, kind, help them understand, explain clearly and so on.

Involve the children in decision making

Both the classroom and its layout are important. If it's too hot or too cold, too cramped and cluttered or simply too dull and uncomfortable, you are getting things off to a bad start. Involve the children in decisions about how the classroom furniture is arranged. Let them know that everyone needs to be able to walk round it without shoving past chairs and tables, the teacher needs a clear sight line of each child and each child needs to be able to face the teacher in a central spot, by turning their chair round if necessary.

Do you seek the children's suggestions for the things you display on your walls? Do the displays reflect their interests, enthusiasms and needs or are they just fancy wallpaper to please inspectors? Why not ask the children what they would like on their walls – within reason – and make sure they help display their choices?

Once you have a physical environment that has included them and taken account of their needs it is your behaviour that sets the tone.

Rewards and sanctions

The gradation of rewards is determined partly by the school, but you will have some leeway to personalise this within your own class. It is easy to think that a teacher's behaviour management begins and ends with the school's behaviour policy, but it is much more subtle than that. Children's behaviour is influenced by what the teacher does and what the teacher says, before you even get down to specific sanctions.

Your look

Is your body language warm and welcoming? Do you stand round shouldered and sluggish when addressing them or do you give an impression of eagerness and enthusiasm, excitement even?

Do you smile at them? Not an inane grin, but anything from a simple raising of the corners of your mouth to a full-on, beaming, toothy grin? Smiles are important in schools, as in life.

Smiles are important in schools, as in life

Even as adults we find meeting smiley people disarming. If we meet someone who is frowning, we know we are not in for a pleasant time. Children need to feel liked in order to feel good about themselves, in order to be ready to learn. With a smile – and forgive me if this starts to read like a cheesy Hollywood musical song – you can soothe, praise, validate, encourage, console and a hundred other things. You are a professional, remember? Even if you have come fresh from a restless night or an argument with a significant other, it is your job to leave that behind at the threshold of the school and give your children the encouragement you get paid to provide. You certainly do not inflict your under-the-weather moods on your children.

A simple thumbs up from the teacher is another non-verbal way of telling a child he is doing well, is on the right track, has your approval. A nod of the head signifies agreement and much more. All of these non-verbal acts are giving the children the approbation that the majority of them crave.

brilliant tip

Use your voice – its tone, dynamics, pitch and timbre all signify almost as much as the words you speak. Think of it at the extremes for a moment with the phrase, 'Well done, Iman!' If you say it in a flat, unenthusiastic monotone or, worse still, ironically, its effect is decimated. Go up the scale a little – say it quietly but with an emphasis on the first two words, and it will sound better. Add some warmth by dropping the pitch and raising the volume and drawing out the first two syllables and it starts to sound worth hearing. Then add on a smile – you speak differently when you smile, you can hardly help it – add an expressive gesture of the hands and arms and then it becomes a compliment really worth having. It will make the child's day. She will glow, sit up straight, smile back and feel she is able to do the work and will now redouble her efforts to do it even better to get another bit of praise from you. What is more, the children around Iman will have noticed it. They will have seen how good it made Iman feel and they will be thinking, 'I'd like some of that!' and they'll work harder too.

As a teacher your voice is one of your most important resources. Use it well and look after it. Don't be afraid to use a loud voice, just use it sparingly. Maybe at a scary point in a story you are reading, or maybe when you think the children are dropping off on a sunny July afternoon, drop it to almost a whisper then, unpredictably, turn the volume up to 10 for a single word in a sentence.

Never underestimate the power you have to make a child feel special, capable and loved. Equally, never forget how you can also make a child feel terrible. Your words and actions count. Use them wisely.

When I am undertaking lesson observations in schools I often keep a tally of how often a teacher gives positive feedback to the children: a 'well done,' or a 'good,' or even a 'yes'. You would not be surprised to learn, perhaps, that in some classes my tally reaches twenty-odd in two minutes, whilst in others it doesn't get into double figures even after half an hour. Some teachers find it hard to give praise, unless a child does something absolutely exceptional – like splitting the atom in a science lesson or playing 'Flight of the Bumblebee' note-perfect on the descant recorder. *Get over it and start giving praise ungrudgingly left, right and centre, for the small things as well as the big ones.* Your praise and approval is sunshine to these children and, when they are basking in it, their self-esteem will soar and their learning will flourish. At first it may be that you have to do it mechanically – a word of praise a minute, maybe – but soon it will become second nature. All the most effective teachers I have seen do it. It is an essential part of what makes them effective.

brilliant tip

Get a child to do a tally of your praise given, say, over a 15-minute period. There is no harm in the children knowing that you want to tell them how fabulous they are – they may even keep you on track: 'You haven't said anything nice to anyone for the last 10 minutes, Miss!' This is part of working together as a team.

In terms of carrots and sticks – positive reinforcement and negative reprimands – the carrots should be inexhaustible and the stick should be buried in the school grounds never to be used again. Some teachers have an understandable reluctance to doling out carrots ad infinitum, yet nearly always they will work, whereas the stick seldom does. Some children will need only the occasional nibble, whilst others need to be gorged on them. Teachers may say, 'Why should I praise pupil A for completing a single mediocre sentence when students B, C and D have written three sides of beautiful prose?' *The answer is, because student A needs it that way and often the students who need our praise the most are those who 'deserve' it the least.* You are in the business of modifying behaviour so that the whole class can work to the best of their ability without interruption or disruption. As Paul Dix writes in his excellent book *The Essential Guide to Taking Care of Behaviour* (Longman, 2010), 'In 20 years of teaching I have never heard a student complain about being praised too much.' The worst they will think is that you're being rather overenthusiastic.

School behaviour policy

Some of the major decisions on behaviour already will have been made for you. A school's behaviour policy is a public document that sets out to parents, governors, staff and children how good behaviour is to be encouraged and how poor behaviour can be improved. Within the parameters of the whole school policy – and you should never stray from it – there is flexibility for you in the day-to-day encouragement of good behaviour within your class. Remember that behaviour in a school is the collective responsibility of everyone who works there and you should never let a positive or negative act go unnoticed simply because a child doesn't happen to be in your class.

> behaviour in a school is the collective responsibility of everyone who works there

Positive strategies

All brilliant teachers know how important it is to 'catch a child being good' and reward them for it in order to reinforce and promote such behaviour throughout the whole class. Always remember, it is virtually impossible to praise a child too much.

Stickers and stamps

Children love them. They are a badge – a visible sign to themselves and others that they have been rewarded. They are available in all shapes, sizes and colours and children will bend over backwards to do something to earn them – even the most hardened Year 6 child will want one (providing it looks cool enough).

Certificates

Certificates can be given for anything: player of the match, star reader, brilliant writer, great homework, being kind, multiplication tables knowledge, etc. They are a visible sign to parents that their child has done something to be proud of and will adorn kitchen cupboards as a reminder and an incentive for future effort.

Golden time

A special 'choosing time', generally on a Friday afternoon, earned by the individual for the collective benefit of the whole class. You need a tariff: two dozen stickers issued in four days equals half an hour of golden time on Friday. Activities can be chosen by the children – a game of rounders, computer time, a quiz, etc.

Marbles in a jar

A visible measure of good behaviour. Each positive act results in a marble in a jar and a full jar equals golden time.

Big breakfasts

The big breakfast works especially well with older children. It might be given as a reward for all those children who completed all homework well for a whole term. The children are invited to attend school half an hour early to enjoy cereal, fruit, yoghurts, milk shakes and the like as a reward for their efforts.

Music choosing

If you work to the soft strains of music, children can earn credits to be the one who chooses it. They have to explain to the class why the music they have chosen is special to them and what they particularly like about it.

Learner of the week

This is perhaps for those quiet, magnificent middle children who just do their best all the time, or for the reformed disruptive type who has had a good week. It could be represented by a certificate or a symbol, such as a trophy or cuddly toy. It can be presented in a low-key way or with lots of razzamatazz at a weekly assembly, depending on the child's preference. The winner gets to keep the trophy on their desk or at home for the whole week and they get to present it to the next recipient. Winners' names could be entered in a roll of honour which could form part of a wall display and get a mention in the school newsletter or on the website.

Best table

For work or behaviour or a combination of the two. Again, it needs to be symbolised by a trophy of some sort. The peer pressure to work together to get the award can often keep low-level disrupters in line.

Call the parents

Do you contact parents only when children have been badly behaved? Why not call them, write or email them when their child has been good? As a parent, it is so dispiriting when you hear nothing but bad news about your child. Hearing good news means they know you are being fair and consistent and encouraging the behaviour you want to see.

brilliant tip

All rewards and sanctions should be clearly understood and consistently applied. If the children don't understand what triggers them, or if they are awarded – or withheld – for incomprehensible reasons, they will lose their efficacy.

Sanctions

Despite your enthusiastic use of positive strategies, you will still need some sanctions at your disposal. The major ones are determined by the school's behaviour policy, but there are fine gradations you can use in a routine way to ensure brilliant behaviour in your lessons.

The frown

Just as the smile is the most basic – and one of the most effective – of rewards, so the frown can be a warning or a reprimand.

The pause

You are speaking to the class and a child is doing something of which you disapprove. Simply pausing and leaving a silence will be signal that (a) you have noticed and (b) you disapprove.

Naming

In an otherwise industrious class session you notice one child is off task in some way. Simply using their name and nothing else usually will get them back on track. It does not need to be barked or shouted, just say the name aloud and that usually will do the trick.

The move

Simply move to stand near where the poor behaviour is taking place. Again, this signals that you have noticed and that you are ready to act.

Turning a blind eye

This is a difficult one. It can be used, but sparingly, to avoid confrontation, which might escalate the behaviour. For example, you see, out of the corner of your eye, Scott poke a finger into Rhys's thigh under the table. You need Scott to know you are aware, so you position yourself where he can see you and you look at him, maybe in a disapproving way, maybe in a questioning way. Nothing needs to be said, providing the action is not repeated.

Context is important. There can be no set tariff which states that behaviour X will be met with sanction Y. The best behaviour decisions are not mechanical but draw on all your professional knowledge and experience.

🔴 brilliant example

A teacher was walking the corridors and there was a group of boys
filling water bottles at the tap. They had their backs to the teacher and
she heard Michael say, 'This bloody thing leaks!' Two of the boys had
seen the teacher – new to the school – and were looking to see how she
would react, so she could not ignore it altogether but, given the mildness
of the expletive, she didn't want to make a mountain out of a molehill.
Michael turned to see what his friends were looking at and went white
when he saw the teacher standing behind him. This indicated to her that
he recognised he had been caught doing something wrong – recognition
being the first stage in acceptance that he had broken a rule. She asked, in
a calm and even voice, for Michael to go to her classroom and wait for her.
This was enough to indicate to the onlookers that Michael's inadvertent slip
had been noticed and that she intended to take action, so she had already
achieved a deterrent effect. In the privacy of her classroom, however, she
was able to talk to Michael briefly and effectively without having to play
to the crowd. She told him simply that it was not good to swear and –
because Michael was a canny lad from a troubled background where much
stronger profanities were the norm – added, 'If you must swear, at least
have the good sense to turn round to make sure a teacher isn't there.' This
signalled to Michael that she recognised this as a mild offence, but could
not ignore it. He respected her common-sense approach, onlookers knew
she had taken action in a reasonable and unemotional way and honour
was satisfied all round.

There are times when some behaviour should be ignored stra-
tegically, especially if it is clearly attention seeking. You need to
remember the human element – you can apply a sequence of
responses only to a certain extent. Your knowledge of the individual will help you to defuse a potentially difficult situation.

When reprimanding a child try and do it one to one rather than
in front of the whole class. There are several reasons for this.

- If the poor behaviour is attention seeking, and you give it attention by drawing the attention of the whole class to it, then the child has achieved success and will repeat the behaviour you want to eradicate.

- The potential humiliation of being told off in front of their peers may add to whatever simmering discontent caused the disruptive behaviour in the first place.

- A discreet word with the child means that the conversation cannot be overheard *but* the other children can see you doing it and know that you are dealing with unacceptable behaviour.

Confrontation

There will be occasions when a situation rapidly escalates into a confrontation. The danger of confrontation is it can lead to anger and, in your reluctance to step back and lose face, you may make the situation worse.

Confrontations are seldom, if ever, conducive to good behaviour management. Your task – as the grown-up, as it were – should be to de-escalate the situation. If a child is raising her voice you should lower yours. If a child is clearly angry you should be neutral and calming. If a child is emotional you need to be unemotional whilst acknowledging their heightened state. When a child looks physically angry or as if they are about to explode, you need to soften your own body language. Where a child is clearly playing to an audience, remove the child or remove the audience. If a child steps into your personal space, step out of it. If a child is jabbing an angry finger at you, take a step back and don't jab back. Allow the child to speak and do not interrupt. When you speak do so confidently but not aggressively. You may be angry as well, but you cannot show it, as that will lead to an explosion. You are the grown up, you are in control, your aim is to de-escalate the situation to the extent that you can deal with its underlying causes. This is not retreat or cowardice – this is professionalism and common sense.

Sometimes you need help

There are other occasions where you will need help from another adult, a colleague teacher or a senior member of staff. For example, a child has refused to begin a piece of work and, when you have made several attempts to persuade, he retreats beneath the table and starts shouting and banging the underside of it, which is disrupting the class and frightening some children. You gather the children on the carpet and judiciously ignore the offending behaviour, but it seems that the child is getting angrier and may hurt himself. It may be that you need to send for assistance. If you are doing this, a simple message for two children to take will do the trick. (Send two children in case one child gets confused or upset.) Also, give them a range of adults to fetch ('Go and fetch a grown up') rather than a named one, as the children might spend time looking for the headteacher who is not in the building. Do not try to drag the child out from under the table, as that could be classed as assault and will frighten the children further and exacerbate the confrontation.

Restraint should only ever be used as a last resort and where the child is in danger of harming themselves or others.

If a fight breaks out in the playground it is bad practice and ineffective to stand between the warring parties. Always try your voice first and, as a last resort and to prevent injury, pull the attacking child off, by their elbows if possible, as that is least likely to result in a fracture. Again, send two children to fetch a grown up to help you.

There is no shame in asking for help from a senior colleague. It would be worse to struggle on unable to cope but hiding it from others. Colleagues

There is no shame in asking for help

will be all too happy to help and will also be able to offer you further advice on how they have dealt with such pupils in the past.

Summary

The importance of establishing your authority from the start cannot be overstated, as it is far easier to establish expectations methodically than to retrieve a situation that has deteriorated.

Get to know your class before September and, if necessary, draw on the experience of their previous teacher after that date to help you deal with particularly difficult issues.

You cannot drown your children in praise – work at it until you are giving it naturally, freely and regularly. It works.

More difficult children need more praise, even if you think they don't always deserve it. You do it because it works for the benefit of that individual and also for the rest of the class.

Always act proportionately and in context and remember – you are the grown up.

Colleagues are there to help. Dealing with behaviour is the collective responsibility of everyone in the school.

CHAPTER 6

Parent power and the power of parents

n this chapter we learn how to work with parents – even the few difficult ones – and how to manage the thorny issue of homework.

The current government is hoping that some groups of parents will set up their own free schools and is encouraging them to do so with all sorts of sweeteners. Indeed, if parents had the energy, time and expertise to set up their own schools, it might be a fantastically successful initiative. Parents are a child's first – and often best and most influential – teacher. They know more about their child than you can ever hope to and, as such, they are important partners in your efforts to help their child learn.

brilliant tip

Always remember the power of the emotional investment parents have in their children. The slightly odd-looking and irritating and rather badly behaved boy in class 3 who drives you mad every day – he is somebody's son and, whilst he may indeed drive them mad too, he is precious and loved.

Never forget: the overwhelming majority of parents – let us say 99 per cent – are sensible, reasonable, supportive and have their child's best interests at heart whilst recognising that there are necessary restrictions within the education system, not least of which is sharing a class with twenty-odd other pupils. It is fair to assume, therefore, that the overwhelming majority of parents will be right behind you in your quest to give their child the best possible education. They will attend parent teacher meetings, listen attentively and enquire what they can do to help. They will volunteer to assist in class and on school trips. They will help make costumes when you have a special day or a school performance. They will attend your assemblies and applaud warmly at the end. Parents will give up their time and cash to help raise funds through the PTA and will help with lifts when you are travelling to other schools for a netball or football match. At the end of the year they will personally thank you for your efforts on their child's behalf and may follow this up with a thoughtful card and chocolates, flowers or a bottle of something warm and welcome. In short, parents are wonderful and you need to listen to them, communicate with them, value them, enlist their support and never ever lose sight of the fact that – even when there are minor disagreements – both you and they want the same thing: the very best for their child.

> the overwhelming majority of parents will be right behind you

These 'in school' forms of parental engagement have little direct impact on a child's educational achievement, though they do wonders for school-home-community relationships and are therefore very worthwhile. The real power of parental engagement lies in the ethos of the home in valuing and promoting education as intrinsically worthwhile for their children. You can help with this in your communications with parents and give them useful advice on how to help their child make the most of education. Sometimes you need to educate the parents at the same time as educating the child.

Parental engagement in any class is influenced by socio-economic status as well as parents' own experiences of education. Also, parents of some ethnic groups may be less likely to engage automatically with the school. What has to be done in those instances is to offer tailor-made support targeted at specific groups, e.g. literacy classes, parenting skills classes and more informal occasions such as coffee mornings or drop-ins, set up so that hard-to-reach parents do not feel intimidated or over-awed by something as simple as entering the school building.

brilliant tip

Parents who are viewed as hard to reach by teachers often see the teacher as hard to reach. Where teachers make frequent and well-judged attempts to engage the hard-to-reach parents', it is found that the effect on pupil learning and behaviour is positive.

Some of you may have been muttering in the course of reading the last few paragraphs and my paean for parents, 'Wish my school had parents like that – ours are a right pain!' and, indeed, they may be. One per cent of parents, maybe even less, seem to have very eccentric ideas about what is best for their child. Amongst that 1 per cent, there may be even a few who actually are incapable of or unwilling to love and care for their child. You still have to try and work with them. In relation to those parents who, inadvertently or deliberately, neglect or harm their child, the chapter on keeping children safe deals with those sorts of issues. For those parents you simply find unsupportive, inter-fering or antagonistic, read on.

The 'interfering' parent: some problems and possible solutions

The parent worried about standards

This parent seems never to be happy with the work their child is doing for you. They may think it is too easy or too hard, they may criticise your marking and assessment of it, they may say their child achieves a better standard when they work with the child at home.

Do not dismiss their claims out of hand. Take them on face value, even if they are couched in terms that you find insulting or that you feel challenge your professionalism. Look at the detail of what they are saying and examine their claims with an open mind, if necessary, enlisting the help of an experienced colleague: 'Connor's mum thinks the maths is too easy for him – can you have a look and let me know what you think?' If, on balance, you find that the parent has made a valid point, then the best tactic is to own up in as dignified and grown up a manner as possible. 'Thank you so much for drawing my attention to this. I have now moved Connor to a different ability group and hope that you will find the work he is doing much more appropriate.' Then follow it up in a couple of weeks to make sure the work is right for Connor and the parents are happy with it.

If, on the other hand, you are 100 per cent sure there is no case to answer, you need to communicate that, too, and this is generally best done face to face. If you have some trepidation about meeting parents under these adverse circumstances, it is sensible to have a colleague, or even the deputy or headteacher, with you for the meeting. Again, courtesy is paramount if relations are to be repaired: 'Thank you for your comments about Connor's work. I take such things very seriously and hope to explain things to help put your minds at rest.'

Deal with each point in turn, stating why you think they are mistaken or badly informed and give them a chance to challenge and discuss further. It may be that they are satisfied by what you have to say and may even be big enough to apologise for their mistake. It may be, however, that they remain dissatisfied. Asking them, 'What were you hoping to achieve with this meeting?' may get to the nub of the difficulty. It simply may be as they stated in their original complaint or it may be something else: they feel the child is not getting a fair crack of the whip in class, or the child is frightened of you or there are things going on at home that have led to tension and their complaint is just a misjudged way of expressing this. If the problem remains unresolved at the end of the meeting, you need to refer it to the headteacher and tell the parents you are doing so. Even if it is resolved, or partly resolved, you need to keep channels of communication open and maybe set up a further meeting in a week or a fortnight's time.

brilliant tip

'Here I am!'

As part of the getting-to-know-you process, once you know the children who are going to be in your class from September, invite the parents in at the end of the day in July just to say 'hello', so they can meet you and see where their child's new classroom is.

The parent worried about their child being unhappy

Sometimes this will come as no surprise, as you will have noticed this too and, hopefully forestalling problems, will have contacted the parents to discuss it with them. Again, all such claims need to be taken seriously until you have disproved them or addressed them.

Occasionally, however, a parent will insist that their child is unhappy, even though there is not a shred of concrete evidence to support such a claim. This is particularly the case with younger children who experience some degree of anxiety when left by their parent at dropping-off time. If the child is particularly upset as the parent leaves – clawing onto her legs, wailing loudly and weeping in a spectacular display – it is always good practice to call the parent within half an hour to reassure them that their 'little angel' has calmed down and is happily working away in the class. For the parent who is not reassured by this, invite them to come and peer into the classroom – unobserved, naturally – to satisfy themselves that the child is fine.

The parent who is never satisfied

These are nowhere near as numerous as we are sometimes led to believe, but they do exist. The important thing is always to take their concerns seriously, always investigate them with an open mind and always report back to them. If they still are not satisfied and still allege things that you have exhaustively proven to be unfounded, you need to refer their concerns upwards to the head or deputy.

brilliant dos and don'ts

Meeting aggressive parents

Do

✔ Bear in mind your own safety. Make sure you stand so you are close to the exit in case you have to make a tactical withdrawal.

✔ Listen. If the parent is engaged in a non-stop tirade you need to state calmly and evenly, 'I will listen to what you have to say, but you are shouting/being aggressive/abusive and I can't help you when I feel threatened.' Repeat if necessary.

✔ Simply leave if you feel in danger or you simply are unwilling to listen to the harangue any further. Again, state calmly and evenly, 'I am still prepared to listen to you, but am leaving until you are prepared to listen to me also.' Do not hang about having said this, but get out and find a colleague so you are not alone.

Don't

✘ Accept aggression – ever. When faced by an aggressive adult there are some essential don'ts:

✘ Argue back. You need the parent to calm down and arguing

back simply fans the flames. Some teachers find this hard to do, but it is unprofessional to become embroiled in a row. You will get a chance to have your say later.

✗ Close the door to your room. If the parent closes it, try and open it again and simply walk somewhere safer.

✗ Allow yourself to be backed into a corner, always keep an escape route clear, if need be by backing towards one. Do not take your eyes off the aggressor.

Such aggression is very rare, even in schools with challenging parents. The above scenarios relate to unexpected visits. If you have a pre-arranged meeting with a parent whom you think might become aggressive, always alert a colleague and ask for them to be present or at least within earshot.

brilliant tip

Some teachers like to see a parent in the playground at the end of the day to let them know their child has done particularly well. This is great. Others like to see a parent in the playground at the end of the day to let them know their child has been an almighty pain in the neck all day. This is not great. If you have bad news to give a parent, always do it privately and confidentially. Praising their child in public is one thing, damning them in earshot of friends and neighbours quite another.

brilliant example

I may be peculiar in this, but I have a particular loathing for letters from school signed, for example, 'Mr B.J. Stuffy'. It is guaranteed to make me feel talked down to. The only thing worse would be a letter signed 'Mr B.J. Stuffy, BA, MA, PGCE'. This is not *Tom Brown's Schooldays*. Lighten up. A letter signed simply 'Bob Stuffy' would have a neutral, or even a slightly   ▶

warming, effect on me. It would make me feel that Mr Stuffy, or Bob as I now like to think of him, is actually a member of the human race, like me, and not some cold, distant, sneering bureaucrat. Lest you think I am labouring this point, or that I am over-exaggerating the importance of the tone of written communications, let me remind you that every single communication you have with parents – not just written but spoken or face to face – has to communicate the effect you want, which is, 'I'm the professional, but we're all in this together' and not, 'I'm the professional and I shall occasionally condescend to involve you in what we are doing to your child.'

Some teachers, particularly those born in the Jurassic period, feel it is wrong for a child to know their first name. Actually, it matters not a jot. You set out exactly how you want to be addressed by the children (and, apart from some early years settings, this still tends to be 'Mr Stuffy') but do not go down the road of overformality with their parents. Unless you want to be mistaken for a junior manager in HM Revenue & Customs.

Equally bad is overfamiliarity – kissing parents on the cheek whenever you meet them is not the done thing in most schools. You are looking to build and maintain a warm professional relationship – no more, no less.

Communication counts. What you write, what you say, how you behave. You are being watched. You will get it wrong sometimes, though seldom irretrievably. Observe how your more experienced colleagues interact with parents and, whilst maintaining your own style and remaining true to your own character and beliefs, see if there is something they do that you could usefully add to your repertoire.

Know your history

Many people, not just parents, think they know all about school and education. Why? Because they went to school and were educated, of course. Now, I occasionally visit a GP and take the medicine he prescribes, but I wouldn't presume to say I'm a medical man on the basis of that experience.

Parents, almost universally, (and, actually, not unreasonably) base their views on education and schools on what they experienced when going through the system themselves (which sounds like the workings of the digestive tract, unfortunately). Of course, they may have attended brilliant schools, or awful or indifferent ones. The likelihood is that, given the passage of time, the school they attended is different to the one their own children are attending. They will, therefore, have occasional misconceptions and maybe one or two prejudices ('Why did you stop using chalk and slate?') but, for the most part, if you are doing your job well, they will be thrilled at the way education has moved on since they were a child themselves.

brilliant tip

Get out more!

From the outset, make yourself available to parents. If you are a new teacher in the school, they will be wondering what you are like and, the more approachable you are, the more they are likely to give you the support you need. Get out into the playground each morning when they are dropping their children off and be there again at the end of the day when they are leaving. That way you will become familiar to them and them to you.

Some parents may have had an awful time at school. They may have been bullied, or struggled unsupported with learning or they may have had a bad relationship with a teacher ('He insisted we call him Mr B.J. Stuffy BA MA PGCE, all the time!'). In short, they bring all sorts of baggage with them and you need to relieve them of it. You do so by your actions and your words. It is called building up a relationship, a relationship that will benefit children, parents and you. All your communications, all your body language, everything you do will contribute to this relationship, so always be aware of it.

brilliant tip

Some children will have parents who no longer live together, but both parents are entitled to receive communications and to attend such events as parent–teacher meetings, special assemblies and so on. Make sure you remember to include these separated parents.

Parent–teacher meetings

Even experienced teachers can find these meetings nerve-wracking. New teachers may be especially apprehensive. Some teachers – I was one – are particularly wary of meeting parents who are also teachers, in case they are better at it than them! Be assured that most meetings will go well, whilst a minority will go less well. This holds good for experienced teachers as well as newly qualified ones. The only essential is to learn from the experience.

brilliant dos and don'ts

Do

✔ Have some notes to form a basis of discussion. Having made notes in the course of the term on your 'page per pupil' records will help here.

✔ Try to keep to time. Most such meetings are scheduled to last no more than 10 minutes. Make it clear in your initial communication about the event that more detailed, and hence lengthier, meetings can be arranged at a mutually convenient time if necessary. If you look at the parents waiting outside your room for their appointment and you notice previously clean-shaven dads sporting beards, then you have probably kept them waiting too long.

✔ Be positive in what you have to say. Remember my earlier comment about the emotional investment parents have in their children. The child in question might be a constant source of irritation to you: the likelihood is that the parents know about the challenges their child poses, so they don't need their noses rubbing in the fact and may well be dreading what you have to say. Best to focus on positive points and how these can be used as leverage to improve behaviour and performance across the board.

✔ Listen. Some parents will be apprehensive about meeting a teacher and you may have to draw out explicitly their views. Their views and knowledge, however, are likely to be of great help in the job you are trying to do with their child.

✔ Follow up things you have agreed to. If parents ask you to look into music tuition for their child, make sure that you do and get back to parents to let them know the outcome. Put things like this in your diary so you do not miss the follow up.

Don't

✘ Avoid giving difficult messages. If a child clearly is well below average in reading, for example, don't attempt to gloss over it and give the impression that everything is fine. Better to be upfront about reading being a challenge for the child and give the parents some strategies that will support what you are trying to do in school.

✘ Bristle or become defensive if a parent questions something you do. You are the professional and you have to respond in a professional way. Defend and justify your practice by all means but listen carefully: if the parent has a valid point, you are missing a trick if you don't take it on board.

✘ Promise something that it is not in your power to deliver – additional adult support, for example. You are just storing up trouble for later and will lose credibility. You might well agree with their assessment of the situation, but you cannot conjure up additional funding. It is more honest to promise to raise their concerns with the appropriate person. Make sure you do so and note the date and time in your diary and ensure you let the parent know you have done so.

Parent helpers

Good parent helpers are worth their weight in gold, whilst bad ones are far more trouble than they are worth. Any additional, competent adult in the classroom is a bonus and research shows that increased adult contact time with pupils leads to improved progress and higher attainment. The converse is that throwing an incompetent adult into the mix will be counter-productive. Training is essential and often it will be you who has to provide it on the job.

> Good parent helpers are worth their weight in gold

Some schools have a policy of parent helpers not working in the same class as their own child. The reasons for this are obvious in that the child may become distracted (or even embarrassed) by having mum or dad there whilst the parent might become too preoccupied with what their own child is or isn't doing.

A brief note or email at the start of the year asking for helpers should yield one or two positive outcomes. The tendency is for there to be more parent helpers available the younger the child, as many parents return to the workplace once their child reaches the age of seven or eight.

Once you have your cadre of helpers, you need to find and build their strengths, which means offering them some training, depending on what it is you want them to help with.

🔍 brilliant case study

The Reading Heroes

An urban school faced a problem: whilst most parents heard their children read four times a week, as recommended by the school, a few refused to do so. Some said it was what teachers got paid for, others said they had neither the time nor the inclination. This meant that up to 30 children were missing out on parent support in the vital area of learning to read, which, in turn, was impacting on the school's standards in reading.

The English leader put a proposal to the head. She would like to recruit a special group of parents to hear these 30 children read on a regular basis in school time. She would advertise the role and sell it to helpers as a positive thing to do, which would enhance their knowledge and skills as well as those of the children.

Her leaflet appealing for parents to 'become a Reading Hero' went home and, by the start of term, she had recruited (and CRB checked) 15, including a couple of grandparents and several dads who were able to commit to a couple of hours each a week. They were given training (just an hour or so) in the skills involved in listening to children read – when to prompt, when to hold back, reading a difficult word for a child but getting them to repeat it – and so on, and then they were unleashed on the children.

The Reading Heroes were dotted round the school at different times of day and had regular child 'clients' in order to build up rapport with them. The children very much looked forward to this special time – as did the Reading Heroes who actually found it as enjoyable, if not more so, than hearing their own children read.

The children made progress and the Reading Heroes were celebrated in the school newsletter and received a gift at the end of term to show the esteem in which they were held. The scheme is now in its third year and has been adopted by other schools up and down the country.

It is a scheme that brings the community into school, gives adults a way of developing new skills, gaining personal satisfaction from finding they are valued for these skills and, at the same time, giving much needed help to children who might, otherwise, have been disadvantaged by their own parents' reluctance to become involved in teaching them to read.

Parents and homework

Your school will have a homework policy by which you are bound, but here are my views on the matter, which are a little controversial.

Homework, in most forms, usually is ineffective at advancing children's learning. It seldom, if ever, influences assessments or exams in a positive manner. There are a couple of exceptions to this, which I shall come to later, but really very few.

It sometimes seems that the main function of homework is to be a constant source of discontent. Some parents demand *more* homework for their children. Other parents complain there is *too much* of the stuff.

Incidentally, Ofsted has long since absented themselves from judging a school by parents' comments about the homework set, because they realise that, whatever the school's policy, about half of parents will be against it and half for it.

If, as educational professionals, we accept that the most significant factor in a child's learning is skilled adult intervention and support, then we have to acknowledge that, with homework, unless parents or carers are willing and able to help support and supervise them, this factor is noticeably absent. Homework tends, therefore, to be of the treading water variety: doing more of stuff you already know, pages of sums or sentences; or of the learning something new without a teacher to help you variety: thereby setting the child up to fail and leading to frustration all round, which is not the best way to encourage learning.

> the most significant factor in a child's learning is skilled adult intervention and support

Moreover, homework discriminates against the least well off in our society. If you live in cramped conditions, with parents who are working shifts or simply worn out after a hard day's graft, you are unlikely to be in an ideal homework-completing environment. Indeed, the most impressive homework that teachers usually see when it is returned, is that which has been done virtually start to finish by a well-meaning but ill-advised parent.

Teachers can find themselves giving lots of precious time to chasing up incomplete, unacceptable or non-existent homework from their pupils, which, given my assertion that little of it is worthwhile in the first place, is a monumental waste of resource.

brilliant tips

Some things simply have to be learned by rote and it is quite possible to do this without adult support at home:

- A knowledge of times tables facts (and the inverse division facts) is an invaluable asset in terms of mathematical education. They can be learned by heart and be available for rapid recall by pretty much any child (or parrot), irrespective of ability. Not all children will fully understand what they have learned, but they will still have an immensely useful calculating tool in their head which they can call on at any time. Most parents know about times tables. If they went to even a mediocre school themselves, they will have learned some or all of them and certainly will know how to help and encourage their child to acquire them. Learning times tables is that rare thing – perfect homework, where the outcomes are meaningful and where parents cannot do it for the child but can assist them in doing it with no specialist knowledge required and no expensive resources or computers.

- Spellings can be learned at home, too, but these are more problematic. They need to be well differentiated – thereby increasing setting and marking workload for teacher – and, apart from essential high-frequency words, many of them will

▶

never ever be used by children. Vocabulary for your school's modern foreign language can also be learned at home.

● Facts may also be learned by heart: dates in history, formulae in science, data and statistics in geography. How often, though, is such activity required at primary school? Remember, your core activity as a brilliant primary teacher is to enable children to reach an appropriate level in the key areas of reading, writing and mathematics.

Marking of homework is also problematic. It adds to your already considerable workload, but without appreciably advancing the standards that the children attain. What is more, if your school policy is not to mark it – or merely to tick several pages of their written toil – then you devalue the exercise and reveal it for the low-level, meaningless bilge that it all too often is.

The truth is that, after a hard day at school – and, for parents, after a hard day at work or at home – why should families be subjected to yet more of the same in the evening or at the weekend? They need time to be a family together. Time to chat, to cook and eat and simply be together. Homework can all too often add further tensions and stresses to what might already be a fraught family life. Release yourself and them from the tyranny of homework and educate them in the few types of homework that actually have an impact, not just cosmetic homework that is done more for show than for anything else.

Educating them about the value – or lack of value – of schoolwork done at home is tremendously important because parents and teachers have been brainwashed by years of tradition into believing that more homework equals better learning. It does not. There is no research evidence to support this point of view and lots of research evidence to oppose it. Homework – like working all day in complete silence, corporal punishment and psychopathic, bullying teachers – should be consigned to the pages of Victorian novels, not forward thinking primary schools in the twenty-first century.

brilliant tip

In order to get parents' support for learning, keep them informed about what their child will be studying by sending home details of the following term's curriculum, with suggestions for visits, books to read and websites to explore with their child.

Parents and children and reading – the best 'homework' of all

By far the most important homework activity any child can engage in is reading – and that should be promoted as a leisure activity, not by the pejorative nomenclature 'work'. We should read because it is at least as enjoyable as watching TV, blasting aliens on your games console, eating pizza or chatting inconsequentially to friends on internet messaging services.

> the most important homework activity any child can engage in is reading

Promoting reading amongst children (and their parents) will do more to advance their learning than anything else, but it does need promoting. Think for a moment of how some teachers 'promote' reading homework. For the most part, they provide a card that the parent has to sign to prove that their offspring has read for however many minutes required, however many times a week. And that is about it. The card is eventually eaten by the family pet or otherwise disintegrates. Where is the drive to show reading as the foundation of learning and as one of the most enjoyable leisure activities available? Where are the recommendations of the wonderful books that children and their parents are guaranteed to enjoy? Where are the opportunities for them to hear you talk about your passion for reading and to hear you read to them, exciting, sad and hilarious books? Where, in short, is the lure and the passion to ensure that reading becomes an activity of choice and not simply another chore-laden box to tick to satisfy the school bureaucrats?

To be a brilliant teacher you need to educate parents in the absolute core necessity of developing good reading skills in their offspring and then providing them with the wherewithal to accomplish it. This means running workshops for parents on how to listen to children reading so that they encourage not discourage. Reading with a child should be a time of warmth and togetherness, not a time of stress and raised blood pressure. They need your permission that it is OK not to do it some nights – when they or their child is over tired, for example – and they need to know that little and often is better than marathon sessions that eat into their downtime.

brilliant tips

Encouraging reading at home

- Choose a quiet time and place to share a book with your child – 10 minutes is usually plenty.
- If your child comes across an unknown word, tell them how to say it and what it means. Ask them to repeat it to you as they look at it on the page. Do not build up frustration by always asking them to build it up using phonics knowledge. Life is too short to sound out every word.
- Boost confidence by using words of encouragement. If a child gets a word wrong, simply suggest, 'Let's say it together' and help them, rather than barking, 'No! That's wrong.'
- Do not attempt books that are too difficult, as this will be discouraging for both parent and child. Build up word power steadily through books that present just a few challenges.

- Little and often is best.

- Talk – briefly – together about the pictures and about the story and characters, if it is fiction.

- Enlist the support of the local library service. Every child in your class should be a member of the library and parents should be given information about the services and facilities the library has to offer.

- Open your own school library for out-of-hours parents and children sessions, where parents can simply find and share books with their offspring with a well-informed teacher or assistant in attendance.

- Produce a one-sided A4 leaflet on the top 10 reading tips for hearing your child read.

- Recommend books for individuals, as well as by age, gender and ethnicity.

- Have book-buying sessions in class in the run up to Christmas. When you ask on the first school day in January, how many children received a gift of a book, you should be aiming for every child to raise their hand.

- Emphasise that, while books are vital, other reading – newspapers, magazines, manuals, catalogues – also has a place. Variety is important in reading.

Pastoral and confidential aspects of working with children and parents

Parents will sometimes give a teacher information that will help them work with their child. For example, if there is a serious illness or bereavement in the family, a marital split or a new brother or sister on the way. They do this because they know that will enable you to support the child through a time of change or turbulence.

Sometimes, you may have to glean this information yourself. If a child seems out of sorts, you might contact a parent or carer to explain what you have observed and what your concerns are and enquire if they know what might be causing it and whether you can do anything to help.

Just as often, a child may reveal to you – and his classmates, if they are in earshot – very personal information about their family. This is because they trust you and it is important to them and they want to share it with you. 'My dad drank beer last night and mum had to lift him out of the hedge when he fell in it,' may be one such gem. Of course, you always respect confidentiality, except in cases where child protection takes precedence.

In many respects, you will be privy to the most intimate details of a family's life, which is a privilege but can also be a burden. Always remember that your primary role is as an educator and you are not qualified or able to take on full time the roles of social worker, counsellor or doctor. You can signpost routes for help for a family who sees you as their first and most amenable point of contact with officialdom (or who simply do not know where else to turn), but never attempt to do it all yourself. There will be support within school for you in these respects and anything you are unsure of, you should share with the headteacher.

Needless to say, you should always adopt a neutral or supportive tone when a parent or child discloses confidential information. You may have strong opinions about what you hear, you may occasionally be shocked, but it is best, on almost all such occasions, to be circumspect about expressing an opinion.

Summary

Parental involvement – helping in class, on visits, fund raising – and parental engagement – helping with learning – are both essential to you in your work as a teacher.

Where parental support is lacking, you can assist them to become involved and engaged and, occasionally, you can get by without them, as in the Reading Heroes initiative. Parents who have bad memories of their own schooling, or whose ethnicity or economic circumstances mitigate against involvement, need extra support and encouragement.

Apart from times tables and reading, most homework is a waste of everybody's time. If, however, it is your school's policy, you have to go with the flow – whilst working to change the policy!

In the area of your work in the classroom, and in the case of homework, it is salutary to bear in mind that you can please some of the parents some of the time, but you are unlikely to be able to please all of them all of the time and, if you try, you will turn yourself into a burnt-out wreck very quickly.

Confidentiality is vital in maintaining good relationships with your children's parents and carers, but you should avoid the pitfalls of taking on their troubles and difficulties as your own. Any issues that may even hint at child protection need to be referred upwards to senior staff immediately.

CHAPTER 7

Standards

I n this chapter we learn how to set and maintain appropriately high standards and expectations and how to set and hit meaningful targets.

Ethos is important. Nurture and caring are important. Nothing, however, is as important as standards.

> Nothing is as important as standards

Your mission as a teacher is to help children learn and you are helping them learn so that they can progress and fulfil their individual promise and, ultimately, have a better life. This, in business parlance, is your core activity – what you earn your salary for.

There has been much written about the drive for standards (accompanied by hated target setting) versus the creative curriculum. In truth, there is no conflict between these two things. In fact, one of the best ways to achieve high standards is to have a creative curriculum – but one with rigour and entirely geared towards improving the learning of all pupils, irrespective of ability, gender or ethnicity.

You can march only with the army you have: starting points

There are two strands to the standards we need to try and address. The first is the value you can add to a child's progress.

The second is the imperative to get each child up to the nationally expected levels at the end of Key Stages 1 and 2 (level 2b and level 4, respectively). This latter has become more important recently because of the emphasis Ofsted is placing on it. Ofsted argues, not unreasonably, that attainment is more important than value added because value added will count for nothing when it comes to the next phase of education and, ultimately, looking for jobs.

This presents teachers with a daunting challenge. If you work at a school where children enter below the average, you have a long and tough job ahead of you to get them to reach nationally expected standards at ages 7 and 11. The good news is it can be done. It is done, in thousands of very good schools, year after year. Hold on to that thought.

The important thing as a class teacher is to keep your eye on short-term, medium-term and long-term progress. For example, if you have received a child in Year 3 who attained level 2b in reading at the end of Key Stage 1 assessment, that child needs to reach at least a level 4b by the end of Year 6 (long-term progress). By the end of Year 3 the child needs to have progressed at least one fine level to 2a (medium-term progress). This means that you have to monitor progress term on term to ensure that the child is on track to attain at least at that level. The phrase 'at least' is important here. Policy will vary from school to school but, as a rule of thumb, children are expected to progress at least two whole levels by the end of Key Stage 2. That is, a total of six 'fine' levels (that is, three fine levels for each whole level, e.g. 3c, 3b, 3a). Many schools expect one fine level progress in Year 3, two in Year 4, another one in Year 5 and two in Year 6. Of course, that is the bare minimum. The true meaning of added value is to improve attainment by more than the expected.

Standards are about *every* teacher, not just those teaching in Years 2 and 6

Sadly, in many schools, those teachers not working in the national assessment years – Years 2 and 6 – can get the entirely misplaced and wrong-headed notion that standards are not *their* responsibility. Nothing could be further from the truth. Success or failure in those year groups are a team effort involving everyone in the school. If everyone does their bit, it is almost certain that standards, when measured by SATs or teacher assessment, will be high. If anyone shirks or otherwise takes their eye off the ball, standards are likely to fall short of the mark. Making sure you do not take your eye of the ball is not a difficult task, but it does necessitate rigour and planning.

Many schools check on pupil progress at least twice yearly. So, for example, in late September you might be asked to list the current attainment of each individual in your class and forecast where you expect them to have progressed to by the following July. Your forecasts will be scrutinised by a senior teacher or the headteacher and may be challenged. Again, taking the Year 3 example, if you forecast that twenty children will make one fine level progress, five will make two fine levels progress and five will, apparently, make none, you are likely to be asked to justify it.

Let us look at the five who apparently are destined to make no progress. You might argue that the assessments at the end of Year 2 bore no relation to their attainment when they entered your class in September and that you would be spending the year ensuring they attained what they were said to have attained at the end of Year 2. Why might this be the case? There are several possible explanations:

- The assessment by the previous teacher was over-inflated.
- The child 'slipped back' during the long summer break.

- The child is coasting and not performing as well as he is able.
- Your own assessment is too severe.

In terms of the first and last points, these issues can be addressed by improved liaison between year groups and shared moderation of work.

---

brilliant example

During the Key Stage 1 SATs/teacher assessment period the previous summer, carried out by the Year 2 teacher(s), the Year 3 teacher should be invited to moderate the work with them. This has several benefits. First, the Year 3 teacher gains familiarity with the standards of work of which the children are capable, which is an enormous help in planning. Second, the Year 2 and Year 3 teachers reach a shared understanding, through moderation, of what constitutes a given level, which will ensure consistency.

As you can see, this system should prevent overinflated or severe assessments. It should also address the notion of the coasting child. If the Year 3 teacher has moderated the child's work at the end of Year 2, she has a very good idea of his capability and can challenge him to work at least at the level he achieved the previous July. There is a further advantage to this form of liaison between teachers. If, in October, you arrange a meeting with the child's previous teacher you can discuss progress. The previous teacher might observe, 'That child is doing better than I would have expected, this child is about where I would have expected and the other child should be doing better.' This may confirm (or confound) your own views. *The important thing is you are engaging in professional dialogue, which helps give you an in-depth knowledge of each child's progress.* You are keeping an eye on the standards ball and your children will stand a very good chance of making excellent progress during their time with you.

And what of the child who seemingly 'slipped back' during the summer break? This is a common and well-researched phenomenon, to the extent that some groups have lobbied for a shorter summer break. My theory is that it is a mirage. A combination of a slightly lenient assessment by the previous teacher in June or July and an overcautious assessment in September by the current teacher leads to this particular anomaly.

Find out where your children currently are

You can base this assessment on the information you should have received from the children's previous teacher, but you can also mediate it through your own assessments in the first few weeks of the autumn term. You need an accurate assessment of where the children are when they enter your class. This does not need to be done by any formal exam. On the contrary, it is probably better done by your own teacher assessment based on work you set for them in the first three or four weeks of term – a piece of writing, some reading exercises and basic assessments in number, shape and space using and applying mathematics. But, if you are a new teacher, what is your benchmark? What should a Year 3 child or a Year 5 child look like in terms of national expectations?

brilliant tip

One thing you can do is moderate your children's work with a more experienced colleague, or someone teaching the same year group as you, in order to establish a full picture of how well the children currently are doing – because this sets the benchmark for the work you have to do by the end of the year in terms of pupil attainment. Moderating work is simply assessing it against agreed criteria and doing so with a colleague or colleagues, so that the judgements you arrive at represent a shared view of what constitutes, say, a level 3 or a level 4. This type of professional dialogue is one of the best forms of professional development a teacher can engage in. It helps establish your ability to level work accurately and will mean that you can assess children both more thoroughly and also more quickly and plan to take them forwards.

Moderating work is something that should be done amongst colleagues at least half-termly, maybe during PPA time or a staff meeting. The idea is that every teacher becomes an expert at assessing and levelling the work that children do. This expertise ensures that the targets you set for the children are based on accurate baselines.

High expectations are the key

As stressed at the beginning of this chapter, every teacher in every year group has a part to play in contributing to a child's progress over a whole Key Stage. It is said by some educationists that every child needs at least three good teachers in a row in order to fulfil their potential. Any dip in the quality of teaching a child experiences will affect their chances of attaining well at the end of a Key Stage, which, in turn, will affect their starting point for the next Key Stage, so they are playing catch up from then on. Success in end of Key Stage assessments is a whole-school responsibility.

> every child needs at least three good teachers in a row in order to fulfil their potential

In the jigsaw of parts that go towards creating high standards you may have good teaching, good behaviour management and imaginative task design. But, if your expectations of the children are insufficiently high, they are not going to make good progress. High expectations need to be based on a good understanding of national curriculum levels and driven by a desire for every child to be challenged to reach their maximum potential. This challenge does not have to be daunting for the children, but they do need to know that in your class only their best is good enough. Clearly, the best work from a child with special needs might not be the same as the best work from a child on the gifted and talented scale. Nonetheless, each child must be supported and challenged always to at least maintain, and more often to improve on, their previous best efforts. This can seem hard on the children at times. It need not be. The way you give messages and the ways you support the children should never be negative. Your messages should instil self-belief and a can-do mentality. Think of it in these terms: if you are overly lenient on a child in terms of expectations and they have a nice, relaxing time in your class but thereafter have fallen behind and struggle to catch up, how exactly have you helped them? I have heard teachers say, 'So and so has such a hard time at home I always try and make up for it at school and try not to push him.' How does that help the child? Children in difficult circumstances often only have one way out of those circumstances – by getting a good education and creating for themselves, through improved qualifications and improved life chances, a better life than might have been indicated by the 'difficult circumstances' they found themselves in.

Research has demonstrated that, if a teacher identifies one child as a high achiever and another as a low achiever, the children tend to live up to expectations. Labels all too often define how we treat people and, invariably, people live up to the labels we apply to them. The American industrialist, Henry Ford, once said, 'Whether you think you can or you can't, you are probably right.' How much better to have high expectations and a can-do ethos that the children can live up to.

⌐ brilliant case study

Informally observing a teacher at work I watched out of the corner of my eye as a child approached her with a piece of writing. The teacher read it and said to the child, 'That is not your best work. I know you can do better than that because I've seen it. I want you to take it away and do it again.' And the child trudged back to his seat.

▶

At the time, though the teacher's manner and tone of voice were perfectly reasonable, I thought it was a trifle harsh. Where was the value of the child's effort? Where was the attempt to ensure that the child had understood the learning goals for that particular lesson? I spoke to the teacher after the lesson.

'I was interested in how you dealt with Ryan's work when he showed it to you.'

'Oh, do you think I was a little short with him?'

'Not short, exactly. Certainly to the point.'

'I know his work well. He has done much better in previous, similar, work and is a very capable writer. My children know I refuse to accept anything that isn't at least as good as their previous best. I plan lessons according to their needs and always give extra help to those children who find it a struggle. Ultimately, though, they have to do the work. If I let them coast because I didn't want to put pressure on them, I would be doing them a great disservice.'

That teacher's class was one of three in that year group and my English manager was in the process of work sampling children's work from all three classes. That teacher's children – mixed ability like the other two classes – were producing written English of a significantly higher standard across the board. Her methods paid dividends for each of those children. She was unwilling to accept second best from or for any of her children and her uncompromising approach meant that they were making great progress. She worked them hard, but she achieved excellent standards.

As a postscript I should add that her children adored her. They would spontaneously hug her in the playground and often come back to see her after they had moved to secondary school. Parents always wanted their children to go into her class and showered her with little gifts at the end of the year.

This notion of a previous best is a useful benchmark for teachers. If a child hands you a piece of work that you are disappointed with, just flick back through their file or exercise book to see how it compares with previous work. Of course, it could always be that the exercise was not well matched to the child but, more often, it will be down to lack of effort or application.

High expectations – the placebo effect

Trials have taken place, which have demonstrated that patients of doctors who are positive and upbeat about recovery from illness, have an appreciably greater chance of making a full recovery than those patients of doctors who are gloomy in their prognostications. Likewise, a high percentage of patients given a placebo (ineffectual sugar pill) that they are told will cure them are, in fact, cured. This is the power of suggestion on the human mind. If it works in medicine, and it often does, then there is no reason why it should not work in learning.

The sports coach who tells his team that they are unbeatable and that the opposition are incompetent, puny second-raters, will often convince his team that they are better than they really are and, consequently, their performance levels are raised and they do go on to win the game.

Similarly, the teacher who tells the class that these mathematical problems are well within their ability is more likely to experience success than the teacher who makes the problem seem insurmountable and unsolveable. Teachers can engender a can-do spirit in their pupils that will give them the confidence to persist, persevere and achieve. Positive psychology works.

Target setting

Setting targets has been a way of life in primary schools for over 10 years now. That does not mean that they are universally liked or even accepted. The so-called 'target-setting culture' has come in for much criticism. Things got a little better when schools began to establish clear starting points for their pupils and forecast what would be realistic, but challenging, expectations for them to reach by the end of Key Stages 1 and 2.

Target setting then became more refined as the obvious became clear: that in order to reach an end of Key Stage target, progress needed to be made in each year of the Key Stage so that the teachers in Years 2 and 6 were not having to play a desperate game of catch up in order to ensure that the children met their targets in that final year.

Tracking systems were set up to monitor children's progress term on term, often using a computer program, to ensure that children remained on track.

brilliant tip

A tracking system simply identifies a child's starting point in terms of national curriculum levels, keeps in sight the necessary end point (the school target) and tracks their progress towards meeting it year on year, term on term. This enables the school to identify those children who are on track to meet their targets and those who are falling behind. Having identified those falling behind, the school, or teacher, can then put in place an appropriate programme of work – possibly supported by additional teachers or classroom assistants – to help ensure that the child catches up before the final assessments.

In this way, children actually are getting a much better deal from their primary education, which is more rigorously focussed on outcomes than ever before. Some teachers still do not like it, saying it is not part of the nurturing ethos that has, historically, been a strength of primary schools. My own view is that targets are a vital part of the primary teacher's work to enable each child to fulfil their potential and work hard to ensure that no child slips through the net or is left behind. But only if the targets are meaningful and not mere box ticking, and that means involving the pupils.

What's in it for me (WIIFM)?

WIIFM is an important element in convincing children of the value of setting targets. Most primary age children are quite compliant and will want to meet their targets to please you, to make their parents proud and to fit in with their peers. The better targets, however, add another intrinsic ingredient, which involves making it clear to the children how achieving the targets will impact positively on their lives and support their ambitions and aspirations.

brilliant tip

Sophie's ambition is to be a nurse. The targets she works towards in maths and science are important because, as a nurse, she will need to be numerate, use measures and understand something of human physiology and the effect of things like exercise and medication on the human body. Her English targets are important because she will need to communicate with people, orally and in writing, and she will need to read to find out about developments in her area of medical expertise.

Ahmet wants to be a plumber, like his dad. His maths target is vital in helping him measure and work out water and gas flow. He will need to work with money. His science will help him acquire a basic understanding of simple physics and get him into good habits of safety. English is important as well because he needs basic writing and reading skills to communicate with customers and to read installation manuals.

By relating the targets to the children's current lives and their future prospects, you can make it more relevant for them and help give them that extra spur to work hard to achieve them. Some teachers make a wall display featuring scenarios like the above for each child and refer to it in the course of lessons to remind the children of the importance and relevance of this learning to them and their lives.

Trainee and recently qualified teachers will be aware of SMART targets – Specific, Measurable, Achievable, Realistic and Time-limited targets. Not only is it important to differentiate targets, you also need to differentiate how you express them. One child will benefit from a brief note written in their exercise book with a broad target, whilst another will need a longer explanation with staging posts along the way. At all times, phrase targets in ways that mean something to the child – not using the jargon that appears in some of the national curriculum documents that were, after all, written by committees in dull and dusty rooms with little real knowledge of the human beings that were going to be at the sharp end of their deliberations.

> phrase targets in ways that mean something to the child

Child-speak targets are essential to add relevance and meaning to what we are asking the children to do. The best targets involve negotiation with the pupil so that they can own them. (The cynic might say, 'If they want to own the targets, photocopy them for them.' Ignore the cynic.) Negotiation doesn't just give owner-ship it helps explanation and understanding.

---

brilliant example

A good starting point for a target-setting discussion is to ask the child simply, 'What do you think you need to do to make this piece of work better?' and then listen to what the child suggests. There will always be something in what they say that you can take, expand on and reflect back to them. Let us imagine the conversation.

Teacher: Read your writing to me, Luke, pausing whenever you put a full stop or comma.

The child reads aloud. There are very few pauses and sentences run into each other.

Teacher:	What do you notice?
Pupil:	There aren't any right sentences.
Teacher:	That's right, well done for noticing that. That's really good because it means you're beginning to get the idea. How could you make sentences out of the words written there?
Pupil:	I need to put some full stops in.
Teacher:	That's absolutely right. Anything else?
Pupil:	Capital letters, too.
Teacher:	Fantastic! Where would the capitals go?
Pupil:	After a full stop.
Teacher:	Which is the beginning of ...?
Pupil:	The next sentence?
Teacher:	Excellent! You are really getting the hang of this. Well done! How are you going to decide where the full stops go?
Pupil:	At the end.
Teacher:	Good, but how will you decide where the sentence ends?
Pupil:	... er, I could read it aloud and, when it makes sense, then that's a sentence and I put a full stop after it.
Teacher:	That's a really good strategy. I think that will work. Can we turn that into a target? What might the target say?
Pupil:	Read my writing as I do it and remember to put in full stops at the end of each sentence?
Teacher:	Excellent! That's a really good target. Can you write it down on your book now, please?

This is a straightforward short-term target and one that will have to be revisited frequently until the strategy becomes second nature to the child, the target has been achieved and the next one can be set in negotiation with the teacher. Of course, not every target-setting conversation will be ▶

as straightforward as the one above and there will be occasions where you have to direct the pupil more. Note that the teacher used lots of words of praise and encouragement in the above exchange. All feedback should attempt to find three positive statements to one that the child needs to work to improve.

In his book *The Essential Guide to Classroom Assessment* (Pearson, 2010) Paul Dix asserts that, 'Useful targets are those that the student creates, drafts and commits to ... It is so much more important that the target is used than whether it is "smart" or not.'

brilliant tip

When the pupil has completed a piece of work, the teacher should assess it only against the criteria it was written against. If the target was, 'To write a narrative using sentences', then the feedback should relate to the child's success in reaching that target. Avoid extraneous but tempting feedback such as, 'handwriting scrappy' or 'lots of spelling errors' – if the child has achieved the target of writing in sentences, hang out the flags and celebrate!

My target is to have fewer targets: manageability for pupil and teacher

Targets are useful when well done and when they have meaning and relevance for the pupil. Always bear in mind, however, how many targets a child can work towards simultaneously. Better to have one important and relevant target than a whole clutch of them, which the child cannot remember let alone achieve.

Some teachers like to write targets in a child's book, others prefer a card on the child's table. The child can then tick off the targets as they are achieved – an important sense of getting somewhere, of making progress. Whichever method you choose, meeting targets is a cause for congratulations and celebrations. Children like to know that what they are doing is important and worthy of praise when they achieve it.

meeting targets is a cause for congratulations and celebrations

brilliant tip

Many targets will be shared by groups of children within the class and this will make it easier for the teacher to plan learning that will help each group without personalising on an individual basis and going mad in the attempt. By grouping children with the same or similar targets, you can focus your attention on several children at once. This also has the added advantage that in those situations children actually gain from the act of working together. Often, they will understand more by seeing how and why a peer struggles and succeeds than by extended one-to-one teacher time.

Parents and targets

One way of celebrating achievement is to share it with parents or carers, either through a message home, or face to face at a termly parent–teacher meeting. Sharing targets with parents also means that, for those that are so inclined, they can help the child work towards the targets at home.

Summary

High expectations are one of the key determining factors in a child's success. Without high expectations of all our pupils, they will never reach their true potential. It is better to have high expectations, even if you do not quite realise them, than to aim low – and miss. For too long this was the fate of far too many pupils, aided and abetted by less than brilliant teachers.

Pupils need to be assessed informally on a regular basis – simply through scrutiny of work – so that the teacher can track, term by term, their progress and address any stalling or going backwards. Teachers always have to have in mind the endgame – the level that child is forecast to achieve at the end of the Key Stage – and make sure they remain on track whilst they are in this class.

Teachers need to moderate work regularly so that there is a shared understanding of 'levelness' within the school. This not only helps keep expectations high but is also first-class professional development through professional dialogue and discussion.

Children should always understand their targets and, as often as possible, should be involved in setting them through a process of negotiation and guidance with their teacher. Parent involvement is also important because their understanding and involvement should lead to their support.

CHAPTER 8

Pupil voice: without scaring the teachers

In this chapter we learn how to make a start, how pupil voice is not about handing over control to the children, how it enhances learning and behaviour and how even pupils observing lessons can be a blessing not a curse.

'The fact is that pupils themselves have a huge potential contribution to make, not as passive objects but as active players in the education system. Students can and should participate, not only in the construction of their own learning environments, but as research partners in examining questions of learning and anything else that happens in and around schools.'

Professor Jean Rudduck

Pupil voice, despite scepticism from some quarters, is not new and is not going to go away anytime soon. In fact, a recent education act has made it law for governors to 'invite and consider pupils' views' whenever they consider change to a school (though at no point does it say 'act upon').

If, however, you don't act upon pupils' views, does it not defeat the object of the exercise? You are not handing over the running of the school to the children – you remain firmly in charge (or as firmly in charge as you ever were). Just as you would consult your colleagues about how to improve professionally,

you are missing a trick if you don't seek the views of the children

you are missing a trick if you don't seek the views of the people who are the focus of all your efforts – the children.

When I was a class-based deputy, back in the Dark Ages before mobile phones and reality TV, I had the bright idea of trying to find out what the children thought of my work as a teacher. I'm sure I wasn't the first to do so, but I was excited at the prospect of doing this action research. I came up with a one-sided A4 questionnaire of the children which included such gems as, 'What do you think I teach well and why?' A simple question, but the responses were, in some respects, a revelation to me and caused me to strengthen some aspects of my practice and ditch others.

Ofsted has been writing to pupils following inspections for years. The letters are often stilted and occasionally pompous, but at least they recognise that children need to be included. What Ofsted does, however, you can do better, providing you keep a few simple rules in mind.

First, use all the means at your disposal to listen to the pupils' views: from pen and paper questionnaires, through online or even text message surveys to face-to-face group or individual interviews.

Second, don't embrace pupil voice without thought, or so wholeheartedly that the children are left to direct themselves with no guidance from you at all: 'It's up to you blue group – if you think you will benefit from putting out the fire in the book corner, I trust you entirely.' You are still the teacher and you still have the final say *and* the final responsibility and accountability.

Decide what the pupils should have a voice about: anywhere on the scale between everything and not much – easy things like playtimes, discos, summer fair; more advanced areas relating to Every Child Matters such as keeping safe, bullying and the like. Then the really meaty stuff – teaching and learning.

Finally, pupil voice (PV) needs to be empowering. If you ask children to have a voice, you need to listen to them – not just pay lip service to them. You also need to point out when you have acted on their ideas and, when you haven't, why you haven't. Asda supermarket has a display in its entrance proclaiming, 'This is what you told us – this is what we did about it.' It is important that pupil voice is seen to be participatory and meaningful. If PV is just a talking shop, it will soon fall into disuse.

Pupil voice through school councils

School councils are everywhere – they are the latest must have accessory for schools along with laptop trolleys and water coolers – and in some cases they are, sadly, little more than tokenism. At least one primary school has a pupil junior leadership team, to shadow the teacher senior leadership team. This is an interesting concept and must look impressive on the Ofsted self-evaluation form, but a little bit of me thinks it's carrying the concept too far and for mainly cosmetic purposes. A bit of healthy cynicism about the uses of pupil voice is actually a good thing.

Unless a school council has a direct and measurable impact on the way children learn and are taught, they might as well be disbanded. Yes, there is a place for them to influence grounds development, playtime, special events like sports days and summer fairs. Better if they're actively involved in combating bullying or promoting community partnerships, but best of all when they're active in promoting better teaching and learning.

brilliant tips

How to ensure your school council has a voice

● Give them a clear remit – maybe pastoral or working on Unicef's Rights Respects Responsibility agenda.

- Ensure that they get to attend part of full governing body (FGB) meetings so that they can report directly to them.
- Ensure the FGB has school council as a standing agenda item.
- Ensure the FGB minutes its actions in relation to pupil voice feedback.
- Ensure minutes of school council minutes (with action points) are displayed alongside governing body minutes on the school noticeboard/website.

Making a start

You may well be on the road to becoming a PV teacher already without even realising it. As always when embarking on something new, first find out exactly where your starting point is: audit (or get a friendly colleague to audit) what you already do in your class in terms of pupil voice – you probably do quite a lot, but have never called it pupil voice. For example, using the answers *always, sometimes* or *never,* complete the following analysis.

Do you:

- ask the children how they are at the start of a session?
- use some form of 'circle time' activity to air views and feelings?
- always listen and investigate when they bring tales of bullying or harassment?
- regularly ask them if they understand what you're teaching?
- respond understandingly when they 'still don't get it' after multiple explanations?
- ask them at the outset what they already know about an area of study and what they would like to find out?
- encourage them to talk to each other about their learning? This could be asking them to talk to a partner for one

minute to discuss a science problem solving activity for example.

- find out what they think of the physical space in which they work and give them the chance to make suggestions to improve it?
- ask them what they think you teach well and why?
- ask them what they think you teach less well and why?
- ask a colleague to find out from your children whether they always feel safe and secure in your class?
- ask a colleague to ask your children to itemise the ways in which you value and encourage them?
- ask a colleague to bring along a couple of their pupils to your lesson for them to act as impartial observers?

Do your *always* answers outweigh your *never* answers? There is a hierarchy to the above suggestions. The first three are basic and routine 'How are you?' activities. The next four are 'What do they know and understand?' activities: all good Assessment for Learning techniques and ones that should become part of your lesson armoury. The following three are explicitly about the classroom experience and allow the children to shape the experience of learning and teaching. The final three involve a colleague and can provide powerful professional development, allowing children to feedback within clearly defined parameters, as any observer might.

⟋ brilliant case study

How pupil voice was developed at one primary school in day-to-day class-based work

The school explicitly set out to develop a culture of teamwork and collaboration was systematically developed within class. This was done through routine activities such as group work, class discussions and ▶

projects, and the use of talk partners, where children talk and listen to a partner in short one-minute bursts so they are able to discuss their learning and develop respect for each other's ideas. The explicit statement, 'We're all in this together' was introduced and discussed.

When introducing new topics, teachers discussed them with the class before starting their planning. This is a standard Assessment for Learning (AfL) technique.

The school regards AfL as a key component of pupil voice because it involves children and impacts directly on their learning. Finding out what the children already know and what they would like to learn about means that you don't waste valuable curriculum time teaching them what they already know and can do. The children's ideas were incorporated into planning. Involvement and engagement levels rose, as children were motivated by the learning they helped design. For example, science lessons incorporated children devising the questions around a given topic rather than teachers telling them what they should be.

The school introduced pupil questionnaires, adjusted for age, to find out answers to specific questions about well-being, valuing all sections of the class and, most importantly, what the teacher does to make learning better – or what they do, or fail to do, that makes it less effective.

They videoed pupil interviews. An adviser interviewed pupils about their opinions and feelings about teaching and learning in school. The questions were simple, but probing. 'How did your teacher make it easy for you to learn today?' 'What things slowed your learning down this term?' These videos were then used to train other staff in pupil voice techniques.

The school is currently experimenting with class charters – formulated by the pupils. Children discuss their rights and responsibilities and agree their own 'class charter', which they all sign up to. This will be returned to when the charter is broken. If they have a right to learn and a right to be safe then what are their responsibilities?

They are also trialling pupil lesson observation. More on this later.

Three brilliantly simple ways of hearing pupil voice within your class/school

All children within the school community should have the opportunity to participate.

1 Website message boards allow children to post ideas and views to be seen by all.

2 Your virtual learning environment enables you to conduct polls and surveys in real time, many of which are suggested by the children.

3 The post box system. Children post their thoughts and ideas in the class/school postbox. These are shared and discussed and sometimes acted upon. (It's the old suggestion box idea: be prepared for some less than serious contributions – 'Brandon Gregory has stinky feet' is not what we're looking for from pupil voice.)

Listen to a variety of children

You can listen to whole school pupil voice via assemblies. Divide an assembly of 200 children into 20 groups of 10, with sugar paper and markers to write down their responses to a given issue. You could use questions devised by the children themselves: 'How can we make playtimes/lunchtimes more fun?' 'How can we raise money for charity and also raise awareness?'

You can focus solely on your own class – in discussion or by questionnaire. What is different about the lessons you enjoy compared to the lessons you don't enjoy? Are teacher introductions too long or too brief? What do you do when they're on task that helps/hinders them?

You could look at a sub group – boys, girls, ethnic groups, able children, SEN children – all depending on what it is you want to find out, but probably again focussed on teaching and learning.

You might, for example, want to find out why the girls did less well than the boys in a recent maths assessment: ask them!

What about looking at the faceless, forgotten magnificent middle? Those children who get on with their studies day in day out – not high fliers or special needs, not attention-seeking or charismatic. It is so easy to overlook them and we should not. This will ensure you don't always listen to the same vociferous few. If pupil voice is to be meaningful it has to include the 'forgotten' children too. Every class has them. The children who, when it comes to parents evening, you are embarrassed to realise you know very little about. Just think about your own class – who are the children whose friends you couldn't list, whose hobbies you don't know, whose background you are in total ignorance of? Just because a child is well-behaved, quiet and cooperative doesn't mean you shouldn't give them the same level of attention as the brightest or most challenged or disruptive pupils in your class.

brilliant tip

Research by the DFE has shown that the pupils teachers most need to hear from are the most difficult to consult. They are the ones who, if you engage them, can have the most dramatic effect on the fortunes of a class/school.

Use a variety of methods

Take the children on learning walks, again with a clear focus – what makes a classroom a good place for learning? What stops it being a good place for learning? What things happen in other classes that the children would like to happen in their own? Remember,

brilliant teachers take the best ideas available and make them their own brilliant teachers take the best ideas available and make them their own.

Use paper surveys and votes: hands up; questionnaires; virtual learning environment (VLE) votes online or in class using wireless voting pads (those ones that are used to ask the audience on *Who Wants to be a Millionaire?*).

Also use face-to-face pupil interviews, e.g. with a subject or learning focus. This can be done one to one or in small groups. It can be especially enlightening to interview pupils after lessons – what have you learned that you didn't know an hour ago (if anything)? Trust needs to be built up over time. It is all about gathering information to make teaching and learning better, pure and simple. Remember, you have the final say on which suggestions are taken up.

Within your own class you might ask a trusted colleague to interview the children about their responses to you. It's not compulsory, it might not always be comfortable but invariably it will be interesting and enlightening and aid your professional development.

Pupils observing lessons

This is quite a controversial concept. Ofsted and the DFE are keen, while the professional associations have voiced concerns that pupil voice is being used to legitimise a management perspective and as a crude and inappropriate tool to monitor teacher effectiveness.

I think pupil voice becomes most powerful – and interesting – when the children are able to express their views on teaching and learning in action – providing it is done within clearly defined and understood parameters. Forget all ideas of mini-me inspectors with clipboards and badges. Observations should have a minimum of formality and children need to be carefully coached in what to look for. It might be focussing on one or two aspects, such as fairness and questioning. Does the teacher ask questions of all groups of children: boy, girl, able, less able, etc.? How might you feel if the teacher asked you that question? Is the teacher supportive and helpful when questioning or too stern and challenging?

It is a sensible plan to have a teacher or classroom assistant helping pairs of children with their observations and with how they articulate their thoughts. It's a fascinating and productive process and also helps the children self-evaluate, reflect on and understand their own learning. Their comments are often perceptive and they are naturally positive. Within the confines of your own classroom you have nothing to lose and a lot to gain. Try it! Here are some questions children have used as lesson observation prompts in my school.

- What do you think the children are learning about today?
- Are the children enjoying the work? How can you tell?
- How is the teacher helping the children?
- What else might the teacher do that might help?
- How is the teacher rewarding and encouraging the children?
- Is this room a nice place to be? Give your reasons.
- Would you like to be a pupil in this lesson? Give your reasons.

Remember, I'm not suggesting children are the font of all wisdom. Sometimes they will not be able to articulate their suggestions and observations, plus they can misjudge as easily as any adult, but their views are almost always useful and occasionally invaluable. You, however, retain accountability and should never be swayed into doing something with which you are uncomfortable.

Summary

Done effectively, pupil voice can change and improve the ethos and the quality of teaching and learning in your school.

You remain firmly in charge. You are the teacher. The grown up. Pupil voice is not about abdicating responsibility, nor about giving children everything they feel is a good idea. There simply isn't enough room in the average classroom to accommodate the drinks-vending machines and PSP consoles children might like. It is, though, about listening, discussing, including and valuing. At its heart, it's about being a team. You are the class leader but their views will help inform your key decisions.

Don't run scared. Don't ignore it, dismiss it or pay lip service to it because it scares the hell out of you or seems like political correctness gone barmy. This is an understandable apprehension, but the reality of well-planned and managed pupil voice can be hugely developmental for individuals and schools.

If you ask children's views *be prepared to act on them where appropriate* or be prepared for them to regard the whole exercise as a public relations sop. When Ofsted asked children whether the school listened to them 34 per cent answered, 'Not very much' or 'Not at all'.

Remember, too, that, just as you have high expectations of your pupils, they will have high expectations of you. Children reserve their highest praise for teachers who show faith in them. A superb way to demonstrate faith and trust is by listening to them.

CHAPTER 9

Keeping safe

I n this chapter we learn about the central importance of child protection, how to protect yourself from unfounded allegations and managing the bureaucratic minefield of health and safety.

Keeping children safe is number one on your list of responsibilities as a teacher. You are 'in loco parentis' – in the parent's place – and you have to care for the children's safety as any responsible parent would. And any responsible parent would admit readily, this does not mean wrapping the children in cotton wool, because that would be counter-productive and would leave them ill-prepared for life in the real world, where they have to assess and deal with risks every day.

Much of the work of keeping children safe is down to whole-school policies and procedures and is, in effect, done before they reach you. All staff working with children – including you – will have been CRB (Criminal Record Bureau) checked to ensure they are suitable to be in daily contact with youngsters. The building will be safe by complying with health and safety legislation, and regulations and procedures will be in place to stop children getting out and stop any ill-intentioned adults getting in.

brilliant tip

The key school policies for you to familiarise yourself with are those relating to health and safety and child protection. In addition, there may be particular areas of the curriculum that are considered potentially hazardous – such as science, PE and some visits outside the school – and you need to make yourself aware of policies relating to these, too.

This may seem like a huge responsibility and it is. For the six or so hours every day, five days a week, the children are in your care, that is exactly what they are – in *your* care. Without feeling safe, secure and supported, the children will find it very difficult to learn. You may balk at some of the safety restrictions and some of the accompanying bureaucracy (risk assessment forms spring to mind), but it is actually not terribly onerous and you need to bear in mind that everything is designed to protect not just the children, but you.

> Without feeling safe, secure and supported, the children will find it very difficult to learn

None of this means that what you do with the children has to be so risk-free as to be dull. You simply have to take all *reasonable* steps to ensure that the children are protected. That notion of *reasonableness* is central. Would a reasonable parent allow their child to walk along a beach accompanied by an adult? Of course they would. Would a reasonable parent allow their child to run away from them along the beach with the tide rushing in quickly and the possibility of not reaching safety in time? Of course they would not. Health and safety and, to a large extent, child protection is about common sense and vigilance.

Health and safety

Health and safety (H&S) gets a bad press – sometimes, seemingly, with good cause – but virtually all H&S guidance stems from reasonable risk assessments and/or in response to accidents and events that no one would like to see repeated.

A lot of H&S guidance will deal with the safety of the staff and visitors, which clearly you need to be aware of, but the crucial parts for you, in your role as teacher, are about the practical safety of the children (and yourself), both in the classroom and when out and about.

Some of the regulations may appear absurd. Ever balanced on a chair or table to put up a display? Of course you have, dozens of times. Not allowed! Apparently there are 3,000 injuries every year related to staff in schools putting up wall displays. You do it because it is easier than trekking down to the caretaker's room to get the stepladder (though even stepladders are frowned upon, unless you have been on an accredited 'working at height' course). The regulations are there to protect you from your own apparent recklessness – and to protect the local authority from lawsuits when you complain you broke a limb putting up a display.

You need to be aware of hazards in your classroom: trailing leads and other trip hazards, blocked exits and other sloppy storage practices, electric power sockets (which should all have safety blanks in when not being used), ensuring there is a clear pathway amongst the tables for children to be able to move about safely, and so on. Bet you never realised the classroom was so dangerous!

Likewise with PE and games, where apparatus has enormous potential for injury through misuse, watch an experienced teacher setting out the equipment (or teaching the children to independently lay out the equipment) and make sure the children know how to use rather than abuse it.

Then there are the hazards associated with particular lessons – use of craft knives in art and DT, saws and pliers, equipment for science experiments and so on. One way of dealing with all of this is to make the first such lesson, or the introduction, all about safe practice and then revisit safety information at appropriate points in subsequent lessons. If you are unsure about the safe use of equipment in these lessons, ask the subject leader to show you or, even better, go and watch another lesson where an experienced teacher is using it.

Bullying

What exactly constitutes bullying? Your school or authority will have a definition, but the lines are not always clear: teasing can begin as fun, descend into irritating and finally become unendurable. Talking about what it feels like can sometimes be helpful so that the bully can empathise with the victim and, hopefully, desist from the bullying. If an allegation of bullying is brought to you, it is important that you take it at face value and investigate it fully. If you do nothing, parents and children will lose faith in you. Bullying can be difficult to prove and sometimes children refer to bullying when it is only one or two instances of name calling. Talk to the children about what constitutes bullying behaviour and what they should do if it happens to them. Bullying is less likely to happen if you have established a caring ethos in your class. How you model relationships for the children is very important – the way you talk to them, the way you listen and so on. The charity, Kidscape, does some very good work on preventing/dealing with the effects of bullying. Kidscape is a charity in the UK established specifically to prevent bullying and child sexual abuse. It aims to equip children with the skills and knowledge to keep themselves safe. (More information can be found at www.kidscape.org.uk.)

Stranger danger

The fear of stranger danger – broadly speaking, abuse or abduction at the hands of a paedophile – far exceeds actual instances of it. Teachers have to tread a fine line between making children aware of what is a high-profile, but statistically improbable, threat and terrifying them into thinking that every other adult is a potential menace.

With older children you can state this case plainly, 'Unlikely to happen, but this is what you could do, if it does,' whilst with younger children it is very much the traditional advice of not accepting sweets/lifts from a stranger. Some teachers like to take this further and advise, for example, even if a child knows the person offering them a lift or inviting them into their home, they should decline if they have not specifically received a direct message from a parent/carer.

21st-century bullying and stranger danger

With the growth of the internet – accessible from phones, MP3 players and games consoles, as well as from PCs – children are prey to cyber bullying and electronic importuning. As a teacher, you can educate the children about internet safety, e.g.: never give out a phone number or address; never agree to meet anyone alone whom you have met only on the internet and many others.

At the same time you need to educate the parents. They should never allow children access to the internet except where the parent can monitor it and they should set security on hardware so that inappropriate sites cannot be accessed. You might be surprised at the number of parents who knowingly collude in under 13-year-olds having a Facebook account.

In terms of bullying by text, I would suggest that you arrange for any particularly troublesome numbers to be blocked or, better still, turn your phone off. Bet the cyber bully never thought of that. Foiled!

I do question the wisdom of allowing under 11-year-olds mobile phones and, in any case, these should not be brought to school.

Internet safety for children

Teach your children the SMART guide to keeping safe in cyberspace:

- **S**afe – never give out personal contact details online.

- **M**eeting someone for real when you've only previously met online can be dangerous. Always have your parents present at any such meeting. Online friends you have been talking to for weeks or months are still strangers in terms of face-to-face meetings.

- **A**ccepting emails or attachments from addresses you don't know can lead to unpleasant messages or even viruses on your system.

- **R**eliability needs checking. Online, people might lie about who they are. Stick to chatting to real friends and family.

- **T**ell a parent or carer if someone or something online makes you feel uncomfortable or if you or a friend are being bullied online.

Internet safety for teachers

Any contact, inadvertently or deliberate, with the children on social networking sites is strictly off limits. Certainly, chatting on Facebook or MSN would be an example of foolhardy over-familiarity. Many schools now have virtual learning environments (VLEs), which have their own internal messaging systems that can be monitored. Teacher–pupil exchanges on such sites – strictly work-based – should be fine.

🔅 brilliant example

Despite age restrictions and school advice to parents, you will find that some older primary school children have accounts on social networking sites like Facebook. If they don't, many of their parents will.

Several children arrived at school excitedly one morning, having found Mr Teacher's Facebook page (it is easy enough to search). It was his first year of teaching and he was already enormously popular with the children as a friendly, dynamic and excellent teacher. They were chatting about it in the playground quite openly to one of the senior teachers. She knew the teacher concerned. She also knew that he had a colourful, if entirely consensual, private life that was very graphically documented in photos on his Facebook page.

She immediately let him know what had happened and stressed the importance of using privacy settings on Facebook. Advice which he took immediately, much to the disappointment of the Year 6 class. The headteacher was also informed to pre-empt any comments from parents.

Child protection

Child abuse, in its many forms, unfortunately is not uncommon. It can occur in the most advantaged suburban middle-class schools in the land, as well as the most socially disadvantaged ones. Unfortunately, it is unlikely to be long before you encounter it in one of its forms.

There are several myths about child abuse. One is that it occurs only in poorer households. False. Child abuse occurs across socio-economic classes, although it can be harder to spot (or people are more reluctant to spot it) when a child is from a seemingly rock solid, supposedly 'respectable' middle-class background.

> Child abuse occurs across socio-economic classes

Another myth is that children are most often abused by strangers. False. The majority of abused children are victims of a family member or a close family friend. It is also a myth that only evil people abuse children. False. Some abuse occurs because the carer simply does not have the skills or means to cope – either emotionally, organisationally or financially.

The most damaging myth is that only violent action constitutes abuse. Again, false. Emotional or physical neglect is more subtle and more difficult to spot than other forms of abuse, but can be severely damaging to the child.

brilliant tip

Child abuse is underreported and underdiagnosed. It may be your first reaction to disbelieve, place it to one side, turn a blind eye and, in general, be reluctant to accept the evidence. Try and identify what it is that is worrying you in relation to the child. Think about what might happen if you delay reporting it or fail to report it at all. You are the children's advocate and you should always speak up for them.

Physical and emotional neglect

Neglect, whilst attracting less media coverage than dramatic instances of physical or sexual abuse, is nonetheless extremely serious and distressing for the victim and the class teacher. A child needs security, love, food, drink and warmth – failure to provide these things constitutes neglect.

Signs of physical neglect could include the following.

● The child might be absent from school frequently.

● It might be that the child is dirty and/or smelly, unwashed, wearing dirty clothes or clothes that are just shabby or unsuitable for the weather.

● The child might steal money or food from other children.

● Perhaps the child is not fed properly – no breakfast before school, being the most common instance – or constantly 'forgets' to bring lunch. The child may look small or skinny for his/her age.

● Sometimes the child isn't cared for in other ways: never taken to the doctor or dentist when in need of treatment, for example.

● The child's parents might present as apathetic, indifferent to the child, depressed or otherwise out of the ordinary.

Emotional neglect, though it leaves no physical signs, can traumatise a child as much as any other form of abuse. In class, the child might seek constant attention (by doing good or bad things) because no attention is given at home. Alternatively, the child might present as very timid with low self-esteem and a nervousness with adults. What the child is going through at home could include:

● Constant belittling, shaming and humiliating from the parent or carer.

● Being called names and having negative comparisons to others made.

● Constantly being told that he or she is 'no good', 'bad', 'a mistake'. Or that the parents 'never wanted' the child.

● Frequent yelling, threatening or bullying.

● Ignoring or rejecting a child as punishment – the silent treatment.

● Limited physical contact with the child – no hugs, kisses or other signs of affection.

● Exposing the child to violence or the abuse of others, whether it be the abuse of a parent, a sibling or even a pet.

Lack of growth, even when a child is not actually deprived of food, may be indicative of emotional abuse. This is sometimes called 'failure to thrive'. There is often an increase in growth when an abused child is removed from home.

What to do

If you feel a child is being neglected, one of the first things you can do is discuss your fears with a colleague – someone who has previously taught the child, perhaps, or the headteacher or child protection liaison officer (CPLO) sometimes known nowadays as the designated person. Always go armed with some brief notes – what you have noticed and when – so that you have some detail to add to what might otherwise appear vague concerns.

At this stage you need to judge whether or not to question the child. If you do, it must be only in the most general terms: 'How are you today?' might elicit no response at all, the child might assert they are feeling fine or they might volunteer they are hungry, cold or tired.

In apparently mild cases, the CPLO (usually the headteacher) might question the child further and even invite a parent in to ask them why the child appears unkempt or hungry. Depending on the parents' response, a decision will be made on whether to refer it to social care.

You will, almost certainly, be asked to keep monitoring the situation and it is well to make brief, confidential notes (including dates, times, what you saw and what the child may have said). It is inadvisable to approach a parent off your own bat, no matter how concerned or angry you are feeling. It is also inadvisable to ask leading questions of the child – questions where the answer you are seeking is contained or strongly implied in the question: 'Has mum not given you breakfast again?'

Your notes will be invaluable if social care get involved, as they will want to know when you first became concerned, what aroused your concerns and what added to them.

The difficult thing is to tread the fine line between being unnecessarily alarmist and allowing genuine neglect to continue unchecked. That is why it is always vital to work with a colleague and preferably the CPLO. If in doubt – refer.

Dealing with the emotional effects on you

Your feelings are likely to be anger, helplessness or an ambivalent mix of concern for the child and refusal to believe that the neglect is deliberate. All you can do is observe and report. The reporting is vital. Children over the years have suffered horribly because of the reluctance or failure of people involved with the child to act on their observations. Far better to cry 'wolf' occasionally and risk upsetting or angering a parent, than to leave unreported that which might save a child from further unhappiness, injury or death. Of course, it is possible to be over-zealous and to see neglect where none exists. If you are doing this in concert with colleagues or the CPLO, they – as more experienced practitioners – will be able to reassure you and guide you.

brilliant tip

Your first duty is always to the child. If necessary, you must put their well being above the parents' sensitivities or – rarely – the scepticism of your colleagues. You may be their only lifeline. This is a great responsibility and needs to be dealt with dispassionately, professionally and thoroughly.

Child protection: physical abuse

It is not so long ago that smacking your own child was considered acceptable, providing it was not excessive in terms of force or duration. Now, though, it is completely frowned upon, for the most part. There have even been cases of parents smacking a child on the legs for doing something naughty in the supermarket and being reported to police or social services as a consequence.

Signs of physical abuse

Children do have accidents and get bumps and bruises, but some instances need to ring alarm bells, such as any of the following.

- The child is unable to explain how an injury occurred.
- The explanation is inappropriate – a major injury is described as though it were a minor one.
- Different people hear different explanations.
- Parents are touchy about it (compared to most parents who are usually upset and blame themselves).
- There is a delay in getting the injury treated.

The black eye, the fat lip, the bump on the head would all merit a question of 'How did that happen?', not just from teacher but from classmates, too.

The signs of physical abuse, however, are not always visible under normal circumstances. Bruises, burns, scalds, bites, scratches and the like can be hidden by clothing. When children are changing for PE or games it may be that you notice such a mark and are perfectly right to ask the child how it occurred. This does not mean that every PE session you get the children to line up in front of you so you can examine them for signs of abuse. It is something you do unobtrusively, scanning the room where they are changing without making them, or you, feel self-conscious about it. The child who goes to a quiet corner to get changed simply might like a bit of privacy rather than having anything to hide.

As with neglect, you are looking for patterns. All burns and bite marks should be investigated as a matter of course. Likewise, severe bruising or scratching. Small bruises may, in themselves, seem insignificant. But if the child always has a collection of small bruises, it is worth checking why. The important thing is not to ask leading questions, nor to make the child feel self-conscious or more afraid. For example, 'Were you hit?' is a leading question. 'What happened?' is not.

brilliant tip

Accidental bruises tend to be on bony bits of the body. Non-accidental bruises are most likely on the face, eyes, ears, neck, top of shoulder, chest, upper arms, inner arms, stomach, back of hands, genitals, thighs – front and back – or buttocks.

Of course, some children straightforwardly will name their abuser.

brilliant example

A class of 10-year-olds were getting changed for rounders when the teacher noticed that one of the girls had a large, blue-black bruise above the right knee. 'That looks painful, Sophie, what happened?' To which Sophie replied matter-of-factly, 'Oh, I was refusing to tidy my bedroom, so mum whacked me with a metal candlestick.' The teacher carried on with the lesson and then went to see the headteacher about it. The head questioned the teacher – not the child – as to the location of the bruise, the size and colour, whether the skin was broken and how the child had explained it. The teacher had made brief notes so was able to answer all the questions and had also completed a skin map. (A skin map is simply a drawing of the outline of a child's body so that you can mark in the location of any marks or injuries.) The head thanked the teacher who then returned to class.

The teacher's (very important) role had been fulfilled. Social care was contacted and given details. They had some knowledge of the family and decided they wanted to interview the child straight away in the school. The mother was contacted and asked to attend and the interview took place within an hour. The mother was prepared to admit the attack and confessed she was finding it hard to cope and needed help.

The upshot was that the case was fully investigated, the child was protected and the mother was able to access support. The headteacher   ▶

thanked the teacher for being vigilant and gave an update about what had transpired. The teacher expected the mother to be angry next time they met but, on the contrary, she was quite open and even-handed about what had happened.

Few cases are this straightforward, but it serves to illustrate the process that the teacher has the all-important role of initiating. Most parents will be angry that they have been referred to social services and will let you know it in no uncertain terms.

Lessons to learn from this example:

- Always give the child the benefit of the doubt. The teacher did not dispute the child's version of events, merely noted it down and reported to the CPLO/headteacher. It is this initial report that is so important. If a child makes a disclosure to you and you ignore it then the child just might continue to suffer in silence, not trusting adults to help.

- The headteacher trusted the teacher's version of events. Because the teacher had made a few notes and used a skin map it was not necessary to put the child through the same questions again, thereby adding to whatever shame/anxiety/ embarrassment they were already feeling.

- The teacher received an update from the headteacher. *If you report a child protection issue, it is important that you know it has been pursued. If you think it may have got lost in the system, check what the situation is: you could be the difference between a child surviving or not.*

Child protection: sexual abuse

Children of all ages, girls or boys, can be victims of sexual abuse. Some sexual abuse will leave no obvious physical injury. Children are reluctant to tell of this abuse, so most often it comes to our attention through quite circuitous, tangential routes. Sometimes, this can be when the class are studying sex education.

Children may try obliquely to 'tell' others what is happening: through drawing, play or spoken hints. They are testing the ground. If the response they get is empathic, they may eventually be more explicit in what they reveal. If the response they receive is angry, disbelieving or evasive, they may stay silent about it forever.

When a child is distressed as a result of sexual abuse, they may exhibit some of the following behaviours:

- A sudden change in mood – a placid child may become angry, a gregarious child may become withdrawn.
- Loss of appetite or other change in eating patterns.
- Sleep disturbance, nightmares or vivid dreams.
- Self-harm.
- Aggression and disobedience.
- Lack of trust in adults.
- Requests or attempts to leave home.
- A girl may take on the role of mother in a family, even if the mother is still present.

Of course, there are other explanations for the above behaviours and it is wrong to leap to the conclusion that sexual abuse has taken place when, in fact, the child simply has a phobia about swimming classes every Thursday, for example.

Another giveaway is that sexual knowledge or so-called sexualised behaviour may occur as a result of direct sexual abuse or from observing others or watching pornography. This may manifest itself in some of the following ways:

- Persistent open masturbation
- Precocious knowledge of adult sexual behaviour

- Sexualised play, often aggressive
- Use of 'adult' sexual language
- Fear of men
- Fear of undressing.

Some conditions, such as difficulty walking, pain on urination, soiling or recurrent bed wetting also may be indicative of sexual abuse – but not necessarily so. If a child exhibits one or more of the above behaviours, it is definitely worth talking to the CPLO or a senior colleague about your concerns.

> According to the NSPCC, disclosure of sexual abuse is made most often to a friend or sibling. Of all other family members, mothers are most likely to be told. *Of all professionals, teachers are the most likely recipient of a disclosure.*

One of the biggest reasons for children not disclosing sexual abuse is fear that no one will listen or, if they do, that they will not be believed and that nothing will change for them. That is why it is always, as a teacher, important to take what a child says at face value and investigate it further (or in the case of sexual abuse, pass it to other agencies to investigate further).

it is always important to take what a child says at face value and investigate it further

brilliant tip

As a teacher an important role is to create the conditions and the relationships where children feel secure enough to take you into your confidence. That is why building relationships is such an important skill. By building trust and creating an atmosphere of support, tolerance and mutual respect, you are creating the conditions in which all children are able to feel safe and – when they feel less than safe – they know they can approach you about it and be taken seriously.

Keeping yourself safe

Rarely, but often enough for you to need to know about it, unfounded allegations are made against members of staff. This can be traumatising and can lead to an inability to carry on in the job. The vast majority of children are honest and straightforward (as are their parents) but occasionally – either through a genuine misunderstanding or as a result of vindictive mischief making – unfounded allegations are made. They all have to be investigated. This could mean the headteacher looking into it or, at the extreme, it could involve the police, social services and newspapers. Here are some tips to ensure you never inadvertently put yourself at risk.

brilliant tips

- Avoid being alone with a child. Always have another adult or, if all else fails, a couple of sensible children present. If you have no option but to be one on one, always make sure the door to the room is wide open so there is no hint of secrecy.

- If, for example, you are ferrying children from a sports fixture, never put yourself in a situation (parents taking other children home) where there is only you and one child in a vehicle.

- Never touch a child, even a friendly gesture like a hand on the shoulder could be misconstrued, if not by the child then by an onlooker.

- Never allow children to become over-familiar with you. This is especially a problem for young male teachers in a Year 6 class, where some of the girls will almost certainly hero worship you

▷

or even get a crush on you. The same applies to young female teachers with the boys. Same-sex attractions will also apply.

● Infant children may dash up to you and wrap their arms around your legs in a friendly embrace. You have to respond in a way that doesn't discourage the child for life from showing affection, without leaving yourself open to charges of impropriety. A broad smile, some friendly words and holding the child's hand as you remove it from your waist will normally do the trick.

● Walking down a crowded corridor, always have your hands where they can be seen and avoid brushing against the children.

● Never give out your phone number, address or email to children. Never ever engage in chat with children on instant messaging websites.

These tips may appear restrictive or even paranoid. They are suggestions only. You must judge for yourself how to play it and you may decide that you are going to ignore them. Teachers do and they never come to any harm. Just don't be the exception.

Use of restraint and reasonable force

Your school will have a policy on reasonable use of force and restraint and you should familiarise yourself with it at the earliest opportunity. As a rule of thumb, it is wise not to have any physical contact with children at all. Even innocently placing your hands on a child's shoulders to guide them can result in an accusation against you. The number of allegations made by a pupil against a teacher seems to rise each year and they are very distressing episodes. In extreme circumstances, however, physical contact in the form of restraint is sometimes necessary. If a child is about to hurt or endanger themselves or another, the teacher can intervene reasonably. Sometimes simply standing between the child and their objective (be it another child or the exit door) can do the trick. On other occasions you will have to stop the child physically. You can do this by guiding them away. Grasp their arm at the point of the elbow (inadvertent fractures are virtually unheard of using this technique) and firmly steer them away from the situation.

The important thing to remember is that word 'reasonable' again. When faced with one child sitting on another's chest, pummelling his face with his fists, you just need to get him off – if a verbal order fails then reasonable force is all you have left to prevent further injury to the victim.

Summary

Children's safety is your first priority. Without feeling safe, learning is never going to take place.

Health and safety can seem nit picking, but it is there to protect you from your own recklessness and that of others. This means, sadly, that you won't be able to strap yourself to a platform hanging from your classroom ceiling in order to recreate Michelangelo's Sistine Chapel (at least not without a risk assessment). But you can console yourself by looking at the original on the internet.

The internet can be a hazardous place for children and teachers. Give the children good advice on keeping safe on the internet – and remember to follow it yourself: no chat rooms with pupils and no friend requests on Facebook from them.

Bad things can sometimes happen to children and you may be the person they turn to for help. Never let them down, always be vigilant, but never try to take all the woes of the world on your shoulders. There are child protection procedures to follow that will enlist the support of specialist child protection workers who will look after the interests of such children better than you can.

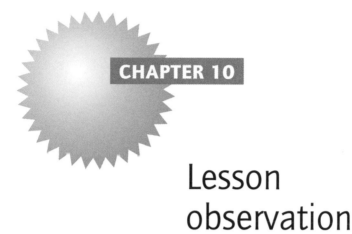

CHAPTER 10

Lesson observation

I n this chapter we learn to embrace, rather than fear, the clip-board-wielding visitor.

Lesson observation! The very words can fill the hardiest of teachers with fear and apprehension. Primary teachers have their own little fiefdom in their classrooms and any other adult in their room can be quite unsettling, especially when they're poised with a clipboard, watching your every move and about to sit in judgement on your professional capabilities. It does not have to be that way.

Constructive feedback on your lessons is one of the best forms of professional development you can have. There is, almost inevitably, an element of threat, especially when the observer is from outside the school – Ofsted or a local authority inspector. What is more, even the most brilliant primary teacher is only human and is capable of having an off day. We all do. The trick is to be able to reflect on your own practice, recognise when your lessons fall below your own high standards, analyse the reasons for any poor performance and plan to eliminate them from your subsequent practice.

One way of overcoming nerves during lesson observations is to do more of them. Yes, really. You may have an aspect of your performance that your own reflections indicate could benefit from improvement, questioning or behaviour management, for example. You could request that a senior colleague comes and observes a lesson and offers their thoughts, first on whether it really is a weak point and second, if it is, what things you might do to improve the situation. You can then return the favour by observing one of their lessons. This is dependent on your headteacher providing time for you to do so, but most heads will be thrilled at the level of professionalism that such a request displays and will be keen to further the type of whole-school learning culture that this sort of activity exemplifies.

If you are apprehensive about inviting a senior member of staff into your lesson, why not ask a colleague to observe you? This has the benefit of adult feedback from a trusted member of staff without the threat that you are revealing weaknesses to someone who may be your line manager or performance management team leader.

brilliant tips

Observe your own lesson

- Set up a camcorder on a tripod in the corner of your class, video your lesson and watch it back later. Analyse plus and minus aspects at your leisure. More than anything you can really notice what children are doing/not doing that may have gone unnoticed when you're in mid-flow. One teacher who videoed a discussion-style lesson commented, 'I would never have noticed the amount of participation – or non-participation – without it. Also, it is really useful to replay to the children so they can self-assess.'

- Ask one or two of your children to be non-participant observers with a clear and simple focus and let you know what they saw. They will need clear instructions as to what to look for, but my experience is that children, especially older ones, are very adept at this.

Who does the observing?

There are several groups who need or want to do observation. Each of these comes with its own stresses and potential pitfalls for the brilliant primary teacher.

● *Ofsted inspector:* this could be anyone from HMI (top professionals) to a non-education inspector or someone who has been out of the profession for a while. Stress levels are likely to be raised because of the high stakes. If your headteacher observes a below-par lesson, you know there will be a further opportunity in a month or so to show how good your lessons can be. Ofsted visits only every few years. Thankfully. Also, with Ofsted, you may be observed teaching three or four times over just a couple of days, so the pressure is really on. Don't be afraid to challenge judgements you think are factually incorrect and let your headteacher know if the conduct of the inspector is either unprofessional or otherwise below standard. Ofsted inspectors are seldom the ogres of legend, most will acknowledge some nervousness on the part of the teacher being observed and make allowances for small lapses.

● *Local authority inspector* (more usually this will be your school improvement partner, or SIP): this should be more comfortable than the Ofsted lesson observation. The SIP usually is attached to a school for at least three years so, as well as knowing all the attainment data, they will be familiar with the school's detailed context and will have more of a developed relationship with staff. The SIP most often will observe lessons informally – dipping into them for 10 minutes or so to 'take the patient's temperature' – or alongside your headteacher in order to check on the headteacher's judgement. The SIP role is to offer detailed, constructive feedback and also to broker support so, if development is needed, you are likely to be pointed in the direction of a useful training course, a teacher in another school or your own, from whom you could learn.

- *Headteacher/deputy/senior teacher*: this group will observe your lessons more often than anyone else. It is part of their role to monitor and evaluate the quality of teaching in the school to ensure standards remain as high as possible. Their feedback will be detailed and supportive and, though they will report to governors the percentage of outstanding/good/satisfactory/ unsatisfactory lessons they see in the school, you will not be identified by name. They will also know you – warts and all – and have a professional duty to support you in maintaining your high standards or in improving them. Headteachers want you to do well.

> Headteachers want you to do well

- *Colleague*: it may be a subject leader looking at how well the subject is taught in the school or a colleague supporting you (your induction tutor in your NQT year, for example) or a colleague you have invited (see above). It may be a colleague who is observing your lesson in order to learn from you and improve their own practice. Either way, this should be relatively stress-free and is a good way to get you used to being observed.

- *Children*: if you are well down the road of pupil voice self-evaluation this type of observation can be enormously empowering for both teacher and child. When pupils act as non-participant observers it demonstrates a high level of trust and excellent classroom relationships.

- *Governor*: thoe who usually are non-education professionals, will have a broad generic brief when visiting classrooms; for example, behaviour or relationships. Some well-meaning governors can overstep the mark, particularly if they have not been briefed properly by the headteacher, and can be critical of some professional aspect of performance of which they have no knowledge. Some may try to chat to you when you're teaching or generally get in the way. The vast majority of governors, however, usually are in awe of the skill displayed by teachers in managing and teaching a class of 30 children. It helps to give them a job/group to work with (keeps them occupied).

- *A student whom you are tutoring*: on this occasion they're meant to be learning at the master's feet, i.e. you. Always use this as an opportunity to get feedback. It's not just you showing the student how it's done, it's a chance for you to learn from an impartial observer what they thought of how the lesson went. One teacher commented that, 'The amount of self-reflection and analysis of your own practice is invaluable. Students ask why you do things the way you do, which really makes you think.'

- *The observed and the observers*: lesson observations are sometimes triangulated between the person observed and two observers. This helps ensure fairness as well as enriching what is gleaned and fed back from the lesson.

brilliant example

As part of the selection process for her first job, a teacher was teaching a Year 3 class with the interview panel observing. The memory stick she had brought was not compatible with the software on the school laptop. She barely batted an eyelid, simply explained the situation to the class and pressed on with a very good lesson minus the technology. Her fluster-free response and ability to adapt and think on her feet helped secure her the job.

Before the observation

Plan for it rigorously and leave nothing to chance. If you know when the observation is going to take place *don't be afraid to seek support*. For example, if you are going to be observed teaching writing and you know you are weak at teaching writing, then seek advice from a colleague who is good at it. Get them to check your planning and where you have pitched the lesson, in terms of the children's abilities, etc. Watch them teach the same lesson and see what they do that you can gain from.

Planning check list

- Is it pitched at an appropriate ability level? Neither too easy nor unreasonably challenging?

- Are the learning and associated activities differentiated to meet the needs of all the children in the class?

- Are the learning outcomes clear?

- Do the activities actually support the intended learning outcomes?

- Are the timings right? Brief introduction, activity, mid-session plenary and formative assessment, further activity and conclusion.

- Have you got an additional extension activity up your sleeve in case the children finish earlier than expected?

Phone a friend – if it's an Ofsted inspection, find out from those who've already been observed that day what the inspectors are like and what they seem to be looking for.

brilliant tips

- Failing whilst attempting an adventurous, calculated, risk-taking lesson is better than failing at a dull, run of the mill, ten-a-penny lesson. Of course, it is better not to fail at either.

- If you know you are likely to be so nervous as to lose the thread of the lesson when being observed, write a script. 'First ... then ... Say 'x', remember ...' and so on: the whole sequence of a lesson. It won't be brilliantly spontaneous, but, if it helps you build up your confidence to the point where you reduce your nervousness, then it will have been worthwhile.

Think about the set-up of your room. Is it the right set-up for the lesson you are about to teach? Use wall displays as part of the lesson, especially where they are based on lessons you have done recently. You could also make display material in the course of a lesson: 'We're going to come up with our own tips on what makes a great opening paragraph to a story and display them on that board so we can refer to them whenever we write.'

Brief children so they don't ask why an observer is there. Also, 'big them up' – 'You are such fantastic learners that they want to come and see you, so show them how brilliant you are!' Children seldom fail to rise to the occasion if you include them in this way and keep them onside.

Check possible outcomes in advance. If you're doing science or maths problem solving, for example, go through it yourself or with your classroom assistant to find possible pitfalls so you can avoid them. Some examples of these are: it's too hard, it's too easy, it will take too long, it won't take long enough, or simply that it doesn't deliver the intended learning outcomes. Best to find out before you teach the lesson!

During the observation

Smile at the children – they want your reassurance. They might be nervous, too.

Think of where you position yourself in the room. Don't forget the nuts and bolts of behaviour management, simple things like ensuring the children are looking at you when you speak and have put pens down in order to show they are paying attention to you. Make sure all resources are to hand, even down to basics like pens, pencils and paper.

Have you made explicit links with previous lessons in your introduction – 'Remember yesterday how we …' and, bridged to subsequent ones, 'Next time, what do you think we need to …', where appropriate?

Ensure you differentiate and extend where necessary. There's always one child who'll say, 'I've finished', 20 minutes before everyone else. You need some form of enrichment/development activity so they make meaningful use of any spare time they have gained.

brilliant example

Give children a chance to go again following your feedback/marking – this is a great Assessment for Learning technique. For example, a child has written the opening paragraph of a narrative. You mark it and detail how it could be improved. The child rewrites it, incorporating the feedback received from you. This means the child gets a chance to have another go while your assessment is still fresh: as opposed to looking at your marking the next day or the next week and wondering what on earth you were looking for.

If the technology (laptop/IWB) falls apart, make sure you don't

You need to think on your feet and have something in reserve that doesn't require a plug and electricity. I maintain, romantically perhaps, that an average teacher with cutting-edge teaching aids is still likely to deliver an average lesson. Whereas, a brilliant teacher with not a resource in site can still deliver a brilliant lesson. It's principally about knowing how children learn, not about how you package the learning or dress it up.

You should be teaching all the time, not marking the previous lesson's work. They will be looking at the number and quality of your interactions. These should be planned interactions due to the excellent planning you've done and not fire fighting because it has all fallen apart.

brilliant tips

- When your lesson being observed begins to crash and burn, despite your meticulous planning, you need to bail out. This may seem drastic – abandoning your planned session for an ad hoc 'up your sleeve' replacement – but persisting with a lesson that has gone badly wrong is worse. You will have shown common sense, flexibility and courage by moving on. In feedback you will be expected, however, to have a detailed explanation of why it did not work and what you would do differently next time.

- Leave an empty chair by the bright children. One inspector once told me, 'Teachers think it's uncanny that inspectors immediately sit down next to the naughty child when they come into a classroom. There's no mystique about it. The naughty children are normally isolated and/or have no one willing to sit next to them, hence there is always an empty chair by them.' If you want to beat the inspector, put the spare chair next to your brightest and most well-behaved pupil.

An observer wants to see interaction: physical, by moving around the space; verbal, by active speaking and listening, and interaction through the use of expression in the face and eyes. This will all be noted, as will skilful differentiation through questioning.

Observers are watching the children as much as watching you and will often position themselves to face the children.

> Observers are watching the children as much as watching you

Remember to check understanding before and during the task: 'Someone tell me what they're doing', 'Share what you've done so far', and address any misconceptions.

Interactive devices, like talking partners, help break up the lesson and aid the children's understanding. (Talking partners: following some input, the teacher will say, 'You have a minute to discuss how you are going to set about this,' and children have rapid discussion with their talking partner. This is an effective technique to use in any lesson.)

Use any supporting adults in the room to the full. During the introduction they might sit with a child who needs prompting or keeping on task. During the activity they might be assigned to a particular individual or group. They could also make notes and assessments of how individuals or groups are doing, which you can then feed back into any plenary. If your classroom assistant is polishing her nails during your introduction, this will not be seen by the observer as a sensible use of resources!

Ensure there is a balance of teacher and pupil talk. Some teachers get so nervous during an observation that they fill any silence – no matter how short – with their own voice. The aim is for the teacher to chair a discussion, not to hog it.

brilliant tip

A technique that children and the observer will like is for the teacher to make deliberate mistakes to check that children are switched on. Just watch their hands shoot up to tell you as soon as they spot it. (Make sure your TA knows you are going to do this so they don't spoil it.)

If an observer comes in midway or towards the end of lesson, will it still be evident what the intended outcomes are? Do a mid-session plenary soon after they come in, in order to recap and make it easy for the observer. The only observers likely to drift in mid-lesson are Ofsted and LA inspectors.

Think of the structure of the lesson – where the key points are, how much learning you can pack in. Recap with the children, 'We've been going for 20 minutes – what have we learned so far?'

Ensure you pose questions to a mix of abilities, genders, etc. This is something you could check with pupil observers – get them to do a tally over a 30-minute period of how many questions you choose boys to answer and how many girls.

brilliant tip

Make sure good answers are lavished with praise   this is part of support and guidance, how well children are encouraged by your teaching. If an answer is wrong, make sure they are clear it is wrong without crushing them – ask other children, 'Why is that answer not right?'

Try and get a discussion going by stepping back from merely repeating children's answers: ask a child, 'What do you think of what so and so said?' The effect you are looking for should be more basketball than ping-pong. In the latter, the discussion merely goes back and forth between teacher and child, in the former the discussion moves about without lots of teacher intervention.

brilliant tip

Make sure your marking is up-to-date in case the observer flicks through the books.

Following the observation

Constructive feedback following a lesson observation is one of the most practical and effective forms of CPD. Ask questions about your feedback and, if necessary (and you're on sure ground), argue the point. You can find out exactly what went well and what went less well and ask for a written feedback or photocopy of the observer's notes. At subsequent observations ensure you have addressed any downsides in the previous one. Ask what support can be provided to help you address any shortfalls and remember observers will not always 'grade' a lesson along Ofsted lines.

Sometimes, when I am giving feedback, I will begin with, 'How was it for you?' and I am looking for a verdict that broadly concurs with my judgement. If they think it was fab and I do not, there is a real problem. From a teacher's point of view that can be quite a challenging question. I would suggest that you come up with one thing that went well and one thing that needs improvement. Then stop. Let the observer tell you their opinions and you can respond accordingly.

Before feedback you should have taken a few moments to reflect on your performance so that you can make the most of the discussion. Have questions prepared: 'I thought things got stuck about 20 minutes in, what did you think?'

Teaching observation as part of a job interview

This is tricky for several reasons. First, you will be teaching a group of children you have never met before – you will have only a vague idea of their ability and little idea of their behaviour. Second, the stakes are high – you want that job. Ask the school whether the children can be labelled beforehand so you can name individuals (excellent for praise but also for behaviour management) and make sure you have five minutes or so to familiarise yourself with the room before you start. Ask the teacher what rewards and sanctions the school uses so you can follow the same procedures that the children are drilled in already.

The school may stipulate what you are to teach, 'A numeracy lesson for a mixed-ability Year 3 class', or leave it open to you. If so, teach to your strengths. If you are hopeless at PE, do not choose this occasion to prove it!

_____

teach to your strengths

_____

Always finish within the allotted time. If you are given 20 minutes, then stop after 19 – if you do 25 you'll see the panel getting restless, as you will be interfering with their carefully planned and tightly packed schedule.

If they have stipulated that you should use technology, do so, but make sure you have a back-up if the technology fails.

Give children the promise of success (also known as bribing them) – verbal praise, stickers, house points, whatever – get them onside from the very beginning of the lesson. One of the smartest things I have seen in this situation was the applicant who, before even introducing herself, had handed out a bright shiny sticker to a child for 'listening well' and for the next 20 minutes every child listened well because they wanted a sticker too.

It is likely that interview observers will be looking less at subject knowledge (difficult to gauge in a 20-minute lesson) than at generic teaching skills: relationships with the children, encouragement, good behaviour management and activities that grab the imagination.

brilliant tip

Always, always, always teach 'up' – that is, show the highest expectations for the year group you've been asked to teach. A

▶

teacher commented on her successful experience, 'If expectations aren't high enough, they just won't want you. If the children find it hard, you can offer extra support in the lesson – or the school will have to reflect on their own standards, but not yours.' If you teach 'down' it is much more difficult to change and adapt.

Summary

Being observed teaching and receiving detailed feedback from it is one of the best forms of professional development you can have.

Observing someone else teaching is almost as good as being observed – you will always learn something, even if it is, 'I wouldn't do it that way'.

Pupil progress is the ultimate criterion of a successful lesson: do the children know more or can they do more than they could at the outset? Have you planned for that?

Always plan with high expectations of the children. Plan for the more able and differentiate down, rather than differentiating up from the less able.

Ensure there are lots of meaningful interactions and never shy away from using the behaviour policy just because someone is watching you.

Make sure the children talk and do more than you do.

Remember, lesson observations are meant to be only an *indication* of how things are going every day. They are a snapshot of a moment in time. If the verdict is 'outstanding', then congratulations! If the lesson is unsatisfactory, it is only a cause for concern if your lessons are regularly unsatisfactory. We all have our off days and you can learn from them: no one ever learned much from getting everything right all the time.

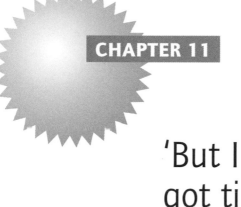

CHAPTER 11

'But I haven't got time to sort out my work–life balance!'

I n this chapter we learn the importance of working to live and we turn our back on living to work.

It is a warm, summer's day. You have just woken up with a start. You are in a comfy chair in the garden, with the sun on your face, looking at the cloudless sky and enjoying the birdsong. You breathe a sigh of relief. Your partner walks across the perfectly manicured lawn with a cold drink for you. 'Thank you,' you smile, 'This is so ... perfect! You know, I've just had this awful nightmare that I was so tired and stressed, I fell asleep during the headteacher's assembly and was snoring loudly.'

'No, dear,' your partner replies, 'This is the dream! You're still asleep in assembly!'

Keeping a sane balance between time spent working and time for you – your friends, family and interests – is one of the great challenges of working life in the twenty-first century, and not just in teaching. Friends who work in continental Europe tell me that their colleagues refer to 'sweatshop Britain' and look with disdain on the macho, long-hours culture at workplaces in this country. Where teaching differs from many professions is in the intensity of the role. In this respect, commentators have compared teaching to acting, with the important difference that actors do a couple of hours' performance a day, whereas teachers are 'on' for six-hour performances daily ('Dahling – I have just had three curtain calls for my science lesson!')

When life is all work and no play:

- you get tired;
- you become resentful;
- your relationships suffer;
- your judgement is impaired;
- you are more likely to suffer frequent minor colds and other ailments;
- you lose the qualities that made you a brilliant teacher in the first place.

Turning up to teach, tired and stressed, means that you are not able to give the children what they really need: a focussed, energetic and inspiring leader of learning. Moreover, things like class control will suffer. You will snap at the children, you will raise your voice, children will sense that they are being picked on and things will spiral downwards. The only thing worse than being a tired teacher is being a hungover teacher. The children will spot it a mile off – you will be akin to a limping antelope wandering into a pride of hungry lions in the Serengeti.

> The only thing worse than being a tired teacher is being a hungover teacher

In looking at the dilemma, we need to keep two salient points in mind: first, it does not have to be this way; second, teachers are their own worst enemies when it comes to achieving this balance.

The best teachers I have known over the years – and some of them have been A1, top-class, bona fide pedagogical geniuses – have always managed to do a superb professional job as well as having a rip-roaring social life. How? They manage their time in a clearly focussed and effective way and protect their 'me' time. This means they prioritise so that the important jobs get done first and the seemingly urgent, but less important, jobs have to wait. They understand the importance of being well-prepared and making the best use of good resources.

brilliant tip

Don't be fooled into thinking that, if you work long hours, you are a brilliant teacher. You are likely to be spending time on things that have little direct impact on children's learning. So work a reasonable number of hours as productively as you can.

One of my favourite figures in business management is Sir Gerry Robinson, who models work–life balance for his employees in that he leaves work at five o'clock daily and believes Fridays were designed for golf. Loud trousers and knocking a small ball with a stick are not really my thing, but I like the principle.

Teachers do not have Friday for golf, but they do have a minimum of half a day a week for planning, preparation and assessment (PPA) and NQTs have a further half day on top of that. Use that time well and it can help prevent work eating into your life.

brilliant tips

PPA time

- Use every minute well. Don't fritter it away making coffee and chatting. Decide in advance what you are going to use it for.
- Set yourself a goal of what you will have achieved by the end of PPA – that way you are more likely to stick to it.
- If you have PPA time with colleagues in the same year group, divide up the work so that you do not all plan maths and all plan English. Let each person plan a different subject, so that you are maximising the time rather than dissipating it.

Just say no!

When there is too much work to do then some of it will have to remain undone. That much is obvious. Some people try to do it all and end up doing a lot of it very badly. Clearly there has to be a minimum, but there is no maximum and you will destroy yourself if you do not set yourself parameters within which to operate. One of the main things you have to do is to learn to identify what is important and then prioritise within that category.

> learn to identify what is important and then prioritise within that category

brilliant tip

Lists can be good. You can itemise what needs to be done and list it in order of priority. Tick each one off as you go which will be a visual reminder of what you have achieved. Don't make huge lists, as long lists don't get done. Concentrate on the next week or two weeks.

Do you need a limo, or will an old banger do the job just as well?

Look at your evenings. How often have you spent two hours making resources perfect for the children? Carefully designed and printed cards, lovingly laminated so that the children will be really appreciative: delightful. But did it actually add to the learning? Remember, you are there to teach and to facilitate the children's learning. All your efforts should be directed to those two aims.

Some of the best resources (in terms of the effect on teaching and learning) I have ever seen have been pulled from a skip. Some of the most incisive worksheets, perfectly matched to the child's ability, have been scribbled down on a piece of A4 on the spot. Think about this. If a child has just completed a mathematics task and you need to extend their learning, why not write down a new activity/set of numbers/shapes on a piece of A4? The point about a worksheet is that it has to serve the intended learning outcome. If it does that, it really is not important whether it looks like a glossy leaflet or shopping list that you have scrawled on the back of an envelope.

The test is in the outcomes for the children. If the outcomes are exceptionally good, then whatever effort you put into it has been worthwhile. If the outcomes are indifferent at best, you have wasted your time. Sometimes an old banger is all you need to get you to your destination – spending time and money on a limousine is not always, or even often, the sensible thing to do.

🔆 brilliant example

A teacher, prone to stress about being observed, had spent days making resources for a lesson that she knew was going to be watched by a senior teacher. The children were going to do some writing and, in order to stimulate them, they were going to do the writing in the role of TV or newspaper reporters. The teacher spent the whole evening before the lesson printing and laminating press cards so that the children would feel like 'real reporters'. They looked fantastic and would have passed muster in any gathering of the ladies and gentlemen of the press. Unfortunately, the teacher spent so much time preparing this essentially window-dressing part of the lesson, that the lesson itself was poorly prepared. The observation took place and the observers rated it only satisfactory because, nice as the press cards were, they added no value whatsoever in terms of the children's learning. The teacher had taken her eye off what was really important in the lesson – children progressing in their learning – and confused show with substance. All that, after devoting an evening of her life to making the resource. ▶

Without being too sombre about it, just imagine your own deathbed scene – at the ripe old age of 120 with all your mental and physical faculties still intact, if that helps. Will you be thinking, as you prepare to face death, 'I'm so glad I neglected family and friends in order to spend an extra couple of hours laminating bits of coloured card that did nothing to help the children learn!'? I think not.

brilliant tip

In your diary block in 'me' time ('me' might be just you, you and a partner, you and a family, even you and the cat) and protect it. Clue: 'me' time can seldom be scheduled between 9 am and 5 pm on a weekday but you can protect a few evenings and a large part of the weekend. You do have to be ruthless about this: it is always tempting to do a bit more, add some polish, etc. but remember – sometimes 'good enough' is good enough.

For those of you so worn down with work that you have forgotten what 'me' time is, how about: eating out, takeaway in, cinema, theatre, drink with friends, gym, sport, dvd complete box set evenings, gigs? Remember them? They should not have to be a thing of the past!

How long do you need to spend resourcing a brilliant lesson?

Here are a few clues. A brilliant lesson does not require whizzy IT effects, every child in period costume, individualised worksheets, a trip to London and all the wonderful things that we do choose to incorporate into lessons from time to time.

The basics for a brilliant lesson are you (the brilliant teacher with good subject knowledge, excellent assessment information and a good command of questioning skills) and some children.

That's it. Something to write or draw on might be useful occasionally, but even that is not essential. Give me a so-so teacher with state-of-the-art ICT equipment, an ultra-modern classroom, top-notch books and a laptop for every child and I'll show you ... a so-so lesson. Give me a brilliant teacher, with no resources other than a halfway comfortable space in which to work, and I'll show you a brilliant lesson.

Some of the best lessons I have ever seen were resourced with whatever was to hand, or with no resources at all. The key to brilliant teaching and learning lies almost entirely in the teacher's skill and knowledge and in the relationship and interaction between the teacher and the pupils. Expensive equipment can add value – the web can bring things like geography and science to life – but is not in and of itself essential.

brilliant tip

Do you arrive at school at half past seven and get reproving looks from teachers who've already been working for half an hour? Do you leave school at 5 pm to looks of disbelief from teachers who will be there till 6 pm? The only important question to answer is, 'Do I work sufficiently long to get the job done well?' and if you can answer 'yes' to that, do not fret about getting into 'who works the longest hours' competitions with colleagues.

Relax. Enjoy your work, but protect your private time too. Get some sleep. Stop taking pride in insane working hours. Forty hours a week is plenty. Decide that you'll do it in less and do it better. Starting today. Make yourself promises and stick to them. Read the chapter of that book by your bed, watch that television programme, listen to that band, bake that cake, call that friend. It is your choice. Do not be your own worst enemy by getting sucked into the macho, long-hours culture.

The wheel is a fine thing and does not require reinventing

Use things that are already available to you. Store up your plans and resources as you make them and save them for next time you revisit that particular area of study. Occasionally they will need tweaking – different children, different abilities – but not wholesale recreation. Do not type them out again – scribble new ideas on them in a different coloured ink. Plans should be working documents not leather bound first editions.

Share with your colleagues – give them planning and resources of yours and freely borrow theirs. This is especially easy to do if you have colleagues in parallel classes – you can divide the planning up between yourselves which can reduce everyone's workload by half or even two thirds.

Make use of online resources, but not indiscriminately – personalise them for your own use. There are many websites that save you reinventing the wheel, but you need to treat them with care. Sometimes they are poorly differentiated or not suitable for your year group. If you are unsure, seek advice from subject leaders in your school.

Many hands make light work

Are you making best use of the human resources at your disposal? Is your classroom assistant utilised to best effect? Are you spending minutes every day (which may add up to hours every week) engaged in tasks that could be done just as well by your TA? Photocopying, collecting slips or money, phone calls about trips: all these things do not require the personal attention of someone educated to degree level. Think also of how your TA can help lighten your teaching load by:

- explaining things for a second or third time to children who need that repetition;

- modelling an activity;
- writing instructions for individuals;
- observing pupils at work and helping you assess their progress;
- marking simple right/wrong answers as they work with a group.

If your TA is inexperienced or (more problematic) has developed bad work practices, you will need to train (or retrain) them. This has to be done sensitively as a poor working relationship with your TA can really add to your stress levels. Make sure your TA is aware of how much you value his or her work, ask for their opinion and advice, include them and make them feel a part of what is going on in the classroom.

Your children, too, are a valuable resource in reducing your own workload. Children can tidy a classroom as well as you can (given the right training). They can create attractive and informative displays under your guidance (and observing H&S measures relating to scissors, staples, glue, etc.) and can even tick simple answers in a maths test, saving you the trouble.

Pace your own workload: restrict 'heavy' marking to a couple of exercises a week and ensure that, whatever you set for homework, does not add to the marking load, whilst remaining meaningful enough to make it worthwhile.

brilliant tip

Avoid initiatives that undoubtedly are attractive but not necessarily worthwhile. It's a tempting idea for your class to enter the Post Office design a stamp competition with those appealing prizes, but where does it fit into the curriculum that you are responsible for delivering? If it doesn't, no matter how appealing, why are you bothering to do it?

Prioritising

Sometimes we are so like rabbits in headlights we lose our sense of judgement and spend time on stuff that apparently is urgent but not particularly important. So how can we sort out the wheat from the chaff and make sure that every hour of our working day is well spent? One way is to subject demands on our time to a simple test of what is urgent/not urgent and important/ not important.

	Important	Not important
Urgent		
Not urgent		

This simple matrix can help you focus on the urgent and the important and leave behind the not urgent and not important. For example:

- Preparing your class for tomorrow's parents' assembly will be both urgent (the deadline is very close) and also important (parents will judge it).

- Preparing a class for a school trip in a fortnight is important (ensure health and safety and maximise learning from the trip), but not urgent (you still have two weeks).

- Tidying your own personal storage cupboard is satisfying – it's easy to do and the results look pleasing – but is not terribly important and is seldom urgent (unless a child has become trapped in the morass of papers and used paper coffee cups and you need to send a search party in). It's a classic displacement activity to put off till tomorrow the important and urgent things you should be doing today.

- A colleague might be badgering you about a course they want to go on with you. It's urgent and possibly important for them, but not for you.

Avoiding the long hours culture

How often have I heard teachers complain that they're in school at 7 am, never take a break and don't leave before 7 pm? Colleagues, they are simply doing it wrong!

- You arrive at 7 am. Make a coffee and chat to a colleague. Log on the internet and check your personal emails. It's now 7.45 am. These activities are fine. They ease you into the day. They're just not *work*, that's all.

- 10.40 am – break time. You sit in the staffroom drinking tea and chatting about the forthcoming sports day. Sure it's work *related*, but it's still a break.

- 12.00 pm – lunch. You haven't prepared for this afternoon's session as you should have during planning preparation and assessment time – you got bogged down in gossip – so you have to dash about sorting it.
- 3.15 pm – school over, you flop down in a comfy chair to unwind then return to the classroom to do some marking. You are interrupted by a colleague who wants to pick your brains about holiday destinations. You happily chat about your favourite holidays and realise it is 5 pm.

See where I'm going with this? It's great to enjoy the 'social' aspects of the workplace, and we all do it to some extent, just don't confuse it with actual work. You have to decide what sort of a day you want: if that decision is to let time slip through your hands in pleasant and relaxing chats with colleagues, that is absolutely fine, but it isn't actual work so try not to moan about the long hours you put in.

Whatever you do, it has to work for you. If it is not working for you then take the initiative and change it.

Who knows where the time goes?

Keep a time log for a day or two and see where the minutes (and eventually hours) get 'lost'. You might be surprised (demerit for anyone who complains, 'I haven't got the time to keep a time log!').

Do it honestly as you go along. Find out where the non-productive distractions happen. Some of them you will want to keep – you're not a robot and need some 'down time' in the working day – others you must ruthlessly excise. Most diaries break the day down into hours. Use this to note each activity you do so that you can tot up the time spent. It might look something like this:

Time	Minutes	Activity
7.50 am	15	Chat to caretaker and colleague; coffee
8.05 am	5	Photocopying
8.10 am	20	Search for netball kits
8.30 am	10	Set up room for science
8.40 am	10	Playground duty
8.50 am	10	Register
9.00 am	80	Teaching
10.20 am	20	Assembly
10.40 am	15	Break; staffroom
10.55 am	65	Teaching
12.00 pm	30	Lunchtime club
12.30 pm	20	Lunch
12.50 pm	10	Set up room for art
1.00 pm	5	Register
1.05 pm	120	Teaching
3.05 pm	20	Home time; chat to parents in playground
3.25 pm	15	Staffroom; coffee
3.40 pm	5	Gathering diary
3.45 pm	75	Staff meeting
5.00 pm	20	Chatting and tidying
5.20 pm	15	Marking
5.35 pm	30	Travelling home
6.05 pm	85	Family
7.30 pm	90	Planning and marking

Break down your daily activities into sections for ease of analysis: teaching, prepping, marking, meeting, photocopying, other admin., and so on. You might also differentiate between the frustration or stress levels associated with each job. Spending 15 minutes on the phone to a concerned parent, unjamming the photocopier, searching in the PE store for a ball pump all take time but are not equally stressful. So add a stress quotient on a scale of 1 (not stressful at all) to 5 (blood-boilingly stressful).

Add up the minutes to a daily (and then weekly) total and see how many minutes were over three on the stress scale and how many under. The next stage is to identify which activities have added most value to the children's learning and which the least. You can also identify which activity gave you the most in terms of job satisfaction and which gave you the least. You can do this simply by highlighting.

From this you can target those areas on which you need to spend less time and plan how you are going to achieve it. Look at how many minutes you spend currently on that activity and identify how many minutes you will save. What can you spend those saved minutes on that will be more satisfying personally or professionally?

brilliant tip

Rather than 'overcoming your weaknesses', which is a drain on your energy, make use of your real talents and passion and leave the stuff you're not very good at to the people who are. This might mean someone else planning your PE while you plan their music lesson, for example.

Every headteacher (and governing body) has a duty of care to staff to help protect them from overwork and stress, so you should find a sympathetic hearing if you can present a convincing case for improving aspects of school organisation that waste time and energy.

brilliant tip

Practise bravery. If you have seven tasks to do but time in which to do only six, one will have to remain undone. You therefore need to prioritise the tasks in order of importance and let the seventh one go. If you have prioritised well, the consequences of postponing that task to another day should be negligible.

brilliant dos and don'ts

Do

✔ Separate home and work. It might be better to finish that pile of marking at school, even if it means staying a little later. Close the door so colleagues know not to interrupt you. That way, when you leave the building, you're not risking internal injury by carrying several kilos of exercise books – and every second is your own to luxuriate in.

✔ Use commuting time effectively. Driving to work you can be mentally prepping your day. Driving from work you can unwind by listening to thrash metal/*The Archers* in the car. Most evenings your working day could end as soon as you close the car door. Make clear dividing lines and stick to them.

✔ Learn from your brilliant colleagues. How do they manage workload? How do they manage to see a band/go to a party every weekend while you're stuck in planning a Design Technology lesson? Ask them!

✔ Recognise that, notwithstanding what I said about separating work and life, sometimes the two happily coincide. I recently watched a team of teachers take on Year 6 children at rounders in a riotously funny ad hoc game after school. The teachers were loving it, as were the children.

▶

✔ Recognise that, however well you manage your time, you still won't be able to do *everything* you want to do either at work or in your home life. Just make sure that the things you do are the most important/enjoyable.

Don't

✘ Get sucked in to the macho long-hours culture that education seems to have imported from business. If someone says to you boastfully, 'I'm the first in school and the last to leave', have the courage to tell them you feel sorry for them and that they're doing something wrong. Unless they're the caretaker. Be proud that you arrive and leave at reasonable times and still do a good job.

✘ Moan about how hard or long you work. It's deeply unattractive to colleagues who will quickly tire of it and you. Work smarter or find an alternative to your current job – a different school or a different career. Moaning is a waste of energy and shows helplessness.

✘ Become isolated. Colleagues will ask you only so often to join them for a drink/coffee after work. You don't always have to accept (see use of time, above) but now and then it's a great way to unwind and bond. (Of course, you could always ask them.)

brilliant tips

● When marking exercise books, get a child to collect them in, open at the appropriate page. It's amazing how much time you'll save not having to flick through every book to find the work you need to mark.

● When you are setting work, for example, writing a story using adjectives, why do the children have to write (and you read and mark) three or four sides? Why not set work which requires the children to write just a story opening paragraph, using adjectives?

Report writing

Writing detailed reports on 30 children is extremely time consuming and really eats into your evenings and holidays – but only if you leave it until the last minute. Here are 10 things you can do to take the last-minute rush out of report writing.

1 Speak to colleagues about how they manage report writing.

2 Collect evidence in the course of the year. Use your page per pupil records to make notes as you go along.

3 Consider giving children a self-assessment ('What I do well/what I need to work on') so you can include their comments in your report.

4 Use your diary to plan a timetable of when you will write the reports so that you spread the load. If your report format is split into subject sections, for example, you might aim to have written all the mathematics sections in three hours spread over one week.

5 When you've written one, show it to the head or senior teacher to make sure it is acceptable in terms of style and content. That way, if it is not, you only have to rewrite one not thirty.

6 Look at examples of existing reports that have been identified as well-written. See what key phrases you can glean and copy them onto Word or a sheet of A4. Have these key phrases in front of you when you are writing your reports.

7 Remember your audience – parents and carers – and avoid using professional jargon.

8 Begin with a positive comment and try to phrase negative ones in a positive way – 'I am sure Archie can develop the self-control needed to listen attentively' rather than, 'Archie has been incapable of listening attentively.' Either way the parent gets the message that Archie is inattentive, but the positive phrase offers hope of improvement which they can then encourage.

9 Always read the child's previous year's report. If you are flatly contradicting the previous teacher's view (which is fine), have your evidence to hand when the parents come knocking at your classroom door.

10 Computer-generated comment banks/report-writing software do not make the process any quicker.

Summary

The worst thing about work and life being out of balance is that you feel you are no longer in control. By managing time in a focussed and effective way and deciding on your priorities you can regain that sense of control. But only you can do it. Don't be your own worst enemy (and everyone else's 'must avoid' person) by moaning rather than taking decisive remedial action.

Make use of your TA, admin. staff and even children to cut down on the time-consuming things that really do not require your level of expertise. If you have built alliances with these people and treated them with the respect they deserve, they can help you.

Avoid seeking perfection in planning, assessment, displays and so on. You will often find that, having spent three hours on a task, it is really not appreciably better than it was after one.

You cannot do everything in the time allotted and remain sane. Learn to distinguish between the urgent and important and prioritise what you have to do. You need to work to live not live to work and keeping a life outside school is a characteristic of the most brilliant teachers I have met. If your life is all work and no play you will become less effective at work and will enjoy it less. Sometimes it is, sadly, the case that you are in the wrong job. Don't struggle on until you have lost all dignity, confidence and energy. Don't ignore your unhappiness. Assess your position and what you can do to make it better. Similarly, don't just quit and do anything else. Plan any departure so that it has a chance of being a successful one.

Do your work to a good standard – acting on the advice of experienced colleagues – and protect a home life through prioritising and accepting that not every job has to be done to limo standards: sometimes an old banger gets you there just as effectively.

CHAPTER 12

Shaping your own future

I n this chapter we learn that your destiny can be in your own hands, how to thrive as a class teacher and how to find and gain promotion.

No one is indispensible. Any organisation should be able to survive the departure of even one of its most important players. But a brilliant teacher should be as close to indispensible as it is possible to get: someone who would be *almost* impossible to replace. This could be because of your specialist skills in one particular area or it could be because of the multiplicity of small roles that you fulfill that forms a crucial part of the school's success.

Making yourself indispensable (1): what schools want from a brilliant teacher

When headteachers are looking for essential qualities in a teacher, first and foremost they are looking for a good classroom practitioner with the potential to become an excellent one. That is the bread and butter. Beyond that, the jam on the bread if you like, they may be looking for expertise and/or leadership in particular subject skills that can be disseminated throughout the school and improve the practice of colleagues to the extent where standards in that subject rise across the board. They might also be looking for someone with broader leadership potential and the capacity to lead a year team or a Key Stage, whom they can develop for internal promotion and thereby improve the leadership capacity of the school.

To be almost indispensable you need to provide things that would be missed immediately if you fell under the number 43 bus, or eloped to Rio with the school secretary and most of the budget. What would the school miss if *you* were no longer there? Don't be modest but do be honest. Without you, would the school founder on the rocks or sail on regardless? Just to help you, here are a few things I would miss in a brilliant teacher (in no particular order):

> To be almost indispensable you need to provide things that would be missed immediately

- Consistently achieves at least good progress with the children across most, if not all, subjects.

- Very well-liked and respected by children and parents.

- Fits in well to the staff team and is well liked and respected by peers.

- Absolutely flexible and never complains about last-minute changes.

- Contributes particular expertise in a subject and acts as a resource for colleagues.

- If someone is missing or a new job has to be done, offers to take on more, whether that be playground duty, clubs, planning, attending meetings – someone who helps to plug the gaps short term and helps to keep the school going through times of difficulty, especially someone who can do it cheerfully. (If someone takes on extra work followed by a strong smell of burning martyr, it is much less satisfying.)

- Someone who brings the headteacher solutions as opposed to problems *or* someone who brings a problem, but also brings the solution to it.

- Someone who notices when colleagues – including the headteacher – are beleaguered and offers, 'I can do that for you!'

This is not an exhaustive list, but just check it against your own performance and attitude and see how you measure up. Would there be weeping at your departure or a brisk, cheery wave goodbye?

Develop intuitive teaching

Intuitive teaching comes about as a result of good subject knowledge, good assessment information, good experience, an ability to be flexible in responding to the children's needs and emotional intelligence. Intuitive teaching is about identifying when a child needs just a little 'nudge' to progress their learning – and then providing it.

🔵 **brilliant** example

A child is working on a task – writing sentences to improve his use of sentence markers. A separate group – slightly more able – are working on sentence connectives. The child puts his hand up and says to the teacher, 'I can use "so" in this sentence, as that would be a good connective.' The teacher responds, 'No, you stick to just writing sentences, the other group are doing connectives, not you.'

This throws up several issues. First, the teacher clearly had not assessed the child's ability accurately or she would have known he was ready to start using connectives. Second, the teacher demonstrated an unacceptable lack of flexibility both in her grouping arrangements and in her response to the child. Finally, she took a child's delight at having discovered some new learning – a real 'lightbulb' moment – and crushed it with her rigidity. There is one golden rule: *every child must make progress. If your lesson plan is a barrier to that, change your plan not the child.* ▶

Let us recreate the exchange as it might have been.

'I can use "so" in this sentence, as that would be a good connective.'

'Yes, you can! That is fantastic! Can you think of any other connectives for your other sentences?'

'I could use "but" in this one?'

'Yes, you could. You are really flying today. Well done. I think you need to move to another group for this lesson so you can show me more.'

Intuitive teachers take risks and encourage progress and innovation. They recognise that their class management systems should always serve the best interests of the children rather than children being shoe-horned into their class management system.

Risk takers shall inherit the earth

Headteachers from the independent sector have complained that new and recently qualified teachers from the state sector are too straitjacketed by formulaic teaching styles to ever be able to produce genuinely exciting lessons (TES, October 2010), and they may have a point. In an age of prescription and top–down targets, teachers (and some of the training institutions) have become risk averse to the extent that they have become efficient but bland.

Brilliant teachers take risks. Calculated, not reckless, ones. They are prepared to throw out the text books and do a bit of daring 'high-wire' teaching and learning instead. Always remember to weigh up when a risk is acceptable and when caution needs to be exercised.

> Brilliant teachers take risks

brilliant example

Dangerous science

This example is not about splitting the atom or recreating the Big Bang, but simply a mode of working when you and the children are tired of doing it by the book.

The teacher begins by telling the children that they are in charge of their own learninq for this session. Their task is to come up with activities that will demonstrate the importance of, and procedures for, fair testing, as though they were designing it for a group of similarly aged children in another class. They have to plan before doing – and take account of resources they will need. Afterwards they have to present their methods to the other groups.

The teacher had taken a deep breath before introducing this because it could easily descend into chaos, particularly in relation to resourcing. In fact, children worked incredibly well, discussing excitedly but thoroughly, listening to each other and contributing, sharing resources and being extremely supportive of each others' efforts.

They learned a tremendous amount by acting as if they were the teachers, planning activities for a class of children, and they learned a lot more about the principles of fair testing than they would have done if the teacher had just led them through a test devised by a teacher.

This is not the sort of lesson you could do every day, but maybe weekly or fortnightly. The more often you do it, the more children will become accustomed to the self-directed learninq that lies at the heart of it.

Become an AfL expert

A surefire way of stimulating discussion and investigation from visual starting points can be found in the web-based resource, Concept Cartoons™.

In science, concept cartoons (www.conceptcartoons.com) can be used as a visual starting point to assess where children are. For, example one cartoon shows three children around a snowman, each making a different statement: 'Don't put the coat on the snowman – it will melt him!', 'I think it will keep him cold and stop him melting.', 'I don't think the coat will make any difference.' Ask the children which of the characters they agree with. This will inform your planning accordingly.

You can adapt this and bring it to life with a group of children in front of the class, each with a statement that the rest of the children can agree or disagree with and stimulate a discussion that will reveal to you the range of levels of understanding throughout your class.

Your starting point is, 'What do the children already know and what do they need to learn?' which is a given on your school's long- and medium-term plans. You know in this particular term in this particular year group the children need to learn about the Second World War. You have decided that on this day in this lesson they are going to learn about children in the war.

brilliant tip

There can be a tendency for inexperienced teachers to think they have to know it all and they will spend an inordinate amount of time reading up on a subject about which they are unsure. The truth is, you do not have to be an expert in everything. Children will like it if you can show that you are an enthusiastic learner too and you will be finding out about a particular subject together. You could even add to your assessment of what the children already know and can do, what *you* know and can do and what *you* would like to find out.

Children can write down on Post-its the questions they would like to find the answers to. This can stay on a wall space and can be used as a form of assessment as you progress through the study, ticking things off and updating as appropriate. It also serves as a reminder to them of what they have already learned.

Having established what the broad classroom knowledge level is, you have decided they don't really know much about what it was like in the air raids, for example. Your planning might start, therefore, getting children to research, using books and the web and maybe also family members, what actually happened during an air raid. You can further define the task by asking for three facts to share with the class. This will help their knowledge of the topic and also their understanding. It will further develop their skill in researching and, in terms of attitude, will foster independence, if working alone, or collaboration if working in a group.

We are now clearly on the second aspect of planning – what will the children do? Doing is important because that's how children learn best, we are told. The 'doing' has to be related directly to the lesson goal – what you want the children to learn.

Finally, after the doing, you need to assess how well the children have met your intended learning out-comes. This can be done most efficiently by oral questioning, referring back to the Post-its and checking understanding. What you learn from this then feeds into the next lesson.

> Doing is important because that's how children learn best

In summary, your written planning can be reduced to the bare essentials of:

- What do they need to learn? (Based on Assessment for Learning and the national curriculum requirements.)
- What do they need to do to learn it?
- How effective was the 'doing' in developing skills, knowledge and understanding?

Leila Walker's *Essential Guide to Lesson Planning* (Pearson Longman, 2008) is an entire compendium of practical and research-based advice on this area.

Making yourself indispensable (2): learning to become a future leader

If you are not currently on the leadership team, ask, for your professional development, whether you might sit in and observe one or more of their meetings. This will be immensely useful in giving you a flavour of what the team actually does and, equally importantly, whether you still want to aspire to be a fully-fledged member of it. It also flags up to the team that you are interested in leadership. By forming alliances with the leadership team you are stating a professional aspiration, as well as gaining professionally from seeing how leadership operates in your setting.

Similarly, look for opportunities to forge links with the local authority (LA) and/or other settings. Initially this may be a matter of 'getting yourself noticed' by LA officers when on courses or taking the opportunity to chat to LA advisors or inspectors informally.

Let me preface this section by stating unequivocally that it is perfectly acceptable to be a brilliant class teacher and not go for promotion.

The expectation is that brilliant teachers climb up the career ladder rather than stay doing class-based work. Why is this? It used to be that going for additional responsibilities in leadership and management were the only ways to break through the salary ceiling, but since the advent of the upper pay scale it is possible for outstanding teachers to increase their salary while staying in the classroom. Salary is not the only motivation, however, as it is also presumed that a really good class teacher will want the higher status perceived with a leadership role.

The fact is that not every brilliant teacher wants to be a leader or manager. They want to teach. Because they are brilliant at it and have no interest in leadership roles because it takes them further away from that day-to-day relationship with a class of children. Some give leadership a try, do it very well, but decide to relinquish it in order to return to wholly class-based duties.

It is also true that not all brilliant teachers make brilliant leaders and not all brilliant leaders were ever brilliant teachers. Saying, 'I just want to be a really good class teacher,' is as noble an ambition as becoming a leader or manager. Some teachers, though, will want to take the next step. They may choose this route for the challenge it provides, for the status, for the higher prospective salary or in order to spread their expertise so that other teachers, children and communities can benefit from it. If you have even a vague interest in whether leadership might be for you, read on.

Look and learn

Initially you will learn about leadership and management from observing the leaders and managers in your own setting. *Warning: this may not always be an edifying spectacle*, so you need to be discerning about the behaviours and attitudes you decide to adopt yourself.

How do your leaders interact with other staff and children? Think *how* things are said as well as *what* things are said. Notice, most of all, what a leader *does*, as actions always speak louder than words. In surveys about what teachers think of headteachers, they always talk about what the headteacher *does* or *has done*, as opposed to what the headteacher has written or said.

Does the headteacher delegate and distribute leadership to others? Some heads like to keep all the leadership power to themselves, not even allowing the caretaker to order new light bulbs without referring back to them. These leaders love the status and authority that comes with being a head and will not easily share that with anyone else. One regrettable consequence of that is they never get to develop other leaders. Working for such a headteacher means that the possibilities to experiment, innovate and develop your career might be rather limited.

Other headteachers are happy to share the limelight and get enjoyment and professional satisfaction from developing other leaders. For them, the best thing about having power is being able to give it away. They are happy to appoint staff as clever or cleverer than themselves, as a consequence of which they are likely to have a highly skilled, stimulating staff, who have the gumption to challenge as well as support the head and keep the school a thriving, dynamic place. One measure of how successful a headteacher is, is the number of other leaders they develop for the community.

Leadership and, in particular, headship gets a bad press and is said to be stressful and daunting. Where several headteachers may gather together at a meeting you may be dispirited at their display of negativity. Headship is an immensely challenging job and it would be surprising if you did not encounter one or two who had become demoralised by the struggle. For many, though, it remains an exciting, demanding and fulfilling career.

brilliant tip

Keep up-to-date

It can be difficult to keep up-to-date with educational issues and initiatives, but, unless you do, in the rapidly changing education world it is easy to fall behind the times. It is worthwhile reading national education journals and the education pages of broadsheet newspapers or their associated websites. This will not only alert you to new initiatives before they arrive but will also inform you about current work – successes and problems – as experienced by schools nationally.

Plan your own future

It is sensible to have an outline career plan in mind. Nothing complicated or even written down, just something to give you markers as your career progresses. A typical plan might be to stay two or three years in your first post before looking for a middle-management post, another two to three years before seeking promotion to assistant headteacher or deputy headteacher and a similar amount of time before applying for a headship.

brilliant tip

If you go on a course for aspiring leaders, you may be daunted by how confident and seemingly better suited to the role everyone else appears. They may tell you they planned, even before college, to take six years to become a headteacher and they are on track to achieve their aim, whereas you may feel you have never planned anything, not even the weekly shopping. Don't let them put you off. If you have the interest, the ability and the perseverance to go for leadership, the likelihood is that you will succeed. Perhaps even succeed more quickly than the ones who have nurtured this ambition since college. The loudest person in the room is not always the most capable.

Think carefully about senior leadership before seeking it

The role of deputy headteacher (interchangeable in some areas with the supposedly lesser role of assistant headteacher) is possibly, by common consent, the most difficult role in a school and one that I would urge you to take on only if you want to take a further step and become headteacher. Deputies have a foot in two camps, as it were – both general and foot-soldier. The workload can be onerous and the difficulties great, especially if you still have a teaching commitment.

Many deputies will attest that, when they are being a brilliant teacher, they find it hard to be a brilliant deputy at the same time. Conversely, when they are being an effective deputy they feel they are less effective as a class teacher. The post is rewarding, of course. In the best schools the deputy will work in close partnership with the headteacher, sharing decisions that will help shape the life chances of hundreds of children. You will learn about headship almost as an apprentice, experiencing alongside your headteacher the ups and downs, pitfalls and pleasures of school leadership, providing you are with the right headteacher. Before you spend precious time completing an application, find out about the school and the head. Visiting is a must. If you have doubts about its suitability for you, go no further with your application. Always make an informed choice rather than simply going for any old job just to become a deputy. I have seen too many promising deputies come unstuck due to a poor relationship with their headteacher. Sometimes this is the fault of the deputy – but just as often it is the fault of the head. (*See the previous section about those heads reluctant to empower others.*)

Building up experience in one school or several

If you can be a sort of David Bowie of teaching and constantly reinvent yourself, experience in one good school can actually be better than experience in several poor ones. If this is the case, it is important that you explicitly draw attention to it in your application.

Ways to reinvent yourself if you decide to stay

● Visit other good schools – arranged as part of your performance management – and introduce best practice from there into your own school: thus are good ideas disseminated.

- When initiatives are introduced, you could put yourself forward to take a major role in trialling and implementing them.

- Show a willing capacity for hard work and regularly offer to do more (and, of course, more interesting) things. But remember your work–life balance. It is possible to do both.

- Become an expert in a suitable field – maths, children's books, writing, ICT, music, sport – many people have advanced their careers by raising their profile through expertise in one area. This does not mean you should have only one string to your bow. You will be a brilliant generalist teacher still, but with the advantage of being an expert as well. Some brilliant teachers become English experts then, when the school needs it, become an expert in science or maths as well.

- Take a lead in planning and running school trips that enhance and enrich the class-based curriculum.

- Think about your unique selling point (USP), which is marketing speak for that thing that distinguishes you from everyone else. It could be a personal quality, brilliant interpersonal skills, expertise in a particular subject or it could be a talent – in sport or the arts – whichever it is, you need to display it to best effect so that not only the children benefit from it but you do as well.

- Be a role model or mentor for new staff. You remember your first day as a new teacher? You know how you felt totally out of your depth till a kind and friendly, more experienced colleague came to check that you were OK, made sure you had what you needed and generally held your hand for the first week or so? That teacher now can be you. There are few more fulfilling things in teaching than helping a new teacher find his/her feet.

- Running parent workshops can raise your profile dramatically as a key player in the school. Governors and

parents will have a view of you and their views count–
ensure that it is a positive one. Remember that, if such
workshops are new for your school and its parents, they
might take several attempts to get off the ground, which
can be dispiriting if you are the person running them. Even
amongst the most reluctant catchment, however, once word
of mouth gets round that you provide a worthwhile input,
their popularity will be assured.

Dip your toe in the water

If you are thinking about taking that next step in your career,
why not look around? By scanning the vacancies, you are not
committing yourself to anything, but it will give you an idea of
what sort of jobs are out there, what they pay and in what sort of
settings. Send off for recruitment packs just to see what the jobs
market is like at the moment. All you are doing is dipping your
toe in the water, after which you can walk away, slowly wade in
or dive in with gay abandon.

By looking at the person specifications (lists of desirable and
essential qualities that the recruiting school are looking for), you
can extrapolate what schools are generally looking for. From this
you can judge whether you already have all the qualities (hurrah!)
or, if not, which ones are the most important to develop. You can
incorporate these into your continuing professional development
(CPD) and also your performance management targets as part
of your review. Make sure that performance management works
for you by preparing for it thoroughly and going into it with
ideas rather than waiting for your reviewer to provide them.

brilliant tips

- If you are in a culture that is in a rut, politely and professionally
  challenge the status quo and suggest and/or trial new ways of

working. Again, making allies is vital to success. If you fall on your face – and who amongst us has not? – demonstrate what you can learn from the experience.

- Try planning a day with no writing implements and enjoy an evening free of marking. Also investigate peer marking and assessment, which is a useful way for children to assess their own work.

- Peer marking and assessment are most easily achieved in maths where, usually, an answer is either right or wrong. It is more difficult in English, but the children can be trained to do so and, in training them, they are also learning about what makes a good written piece themselves.

- Try giving them a piece of writing from last year's class and give them the success criteria. The question you pose is, 'How many of the success criteria have been met and what does this person need to do to improve it?' If they do this in pairs they can share their findings with the class and talk about the pitfalls involved.

- Alternatively, tell them that, 'This is a good piece of writing' and ask them to work out what the success criteria must have been.

- Teachers talk too much. Give the children a chance. When you ask them a question, don't step in and answer it for them. How can they become fluent and articulate when you keep finishing off their sentences for them? A pause, a silence, can be a good thing, if done in an atmosphere of support and encouragement.

What to do when things go wrong

As a brilliant teacher, you do not have to be the font of all wisdom. Just as it is OK to say to your class, 'I don't know the answer to that

The best teachers are always willing to listen honestly and receptively to the views of the people they teach one – let's find out together,' so you should still seek advice, no matter how illustrious or elevated your position becomes. The best teachers, leaders and managers (including headteachers) are always willing to listen honestly and receptively to the views of the people they teach, lead and manage.

If you need to leave, do so on good terms

If the job is just not for you (or you recognise that you are not for the job), you need to exit gracefully and with your professional reputation as intact as possible. Do not wait to be pushed, but, equally, do not go from the frying pan into the fire – choose your next job with greater care, rather than just fleeing the scene of your present misfortune.

brilliant tip

Always seek advice from your professional association representative. The number of teachers who fail to do this never ceases to amaze me. Representatives will support and advise you – they will be honest and open about your chances of success and you would do well to listen to their good advice.

We all make mistakes

No matter how brilliant you become as a teacher inevitably there will be times when you make mistakes and misjudgements and simply get things wrong. This is how we progress – learning lessons from our own failures, be they great or small. When, as is inevitable, you receive advice – which may be couched as criticism – always give it careful consideration, even when your first instinct is that criticism is unfounded. This may seem obvious, but some people, when criticised, no matter how fairly and evenly, resent it and throw their toys out of the pram. Apart from this being unedifying to behold and likely to sow further doubts about your long-term future prospects in the minds of your line managers, you are missing the chance to develop yourself professionally.

✴ brilliant tip

It is always better to take time to reflect honestly before making a response to criticism. If you receive a dressing down, respond in measured terms, but then take 24 hours to consider the criticism. This gives you a chance, away from the initial feelings of hurt, embarrassment or anger, to consider whether what was said was fair and reasonable. If it was, take it on the chin and thank your critic for drawing your attention to something you can now improve.

Similarly, always temper your responses when a problem is brought to you.

▶ brilliant example

A young teacher is told that her teaching assistant (TA) has been posting defamatory messages on her Facebook page, complaining about being given a 'dressing down' by the teacher. This has been read by parents who have joined in with the sentiment and the parent is concerned that this is an inappropriate way for an employee of the school to behave. 'I really think you need to have it out with her!' is the parent's parting shot.

The teacher is angry and upset. She thought she got on really well with her TA and feels hurt by this apparent act of defiance. She cannot even recall giving the TA a dressing down. Despite her feelings, she calmly thanks the parent and tells her she will look into it, deciding to check out the facts for herself before rushing to tear into her TA.

▶

On checking Facebook, she found it contained a very mild remark about having been 'told off' for the first time by an unnamed person at school and a couple of sympathetic, but highly moderate, comments from parents who happened to be friends of the TA.

The teacher was enormously relieved both that the comments were fair and that the reported vitriol from the TA had been exaggerated. She was also relieved – and allowed herself a pat on the back – for not having leapt in feet first as soon as the parent spoke to her.

The main lesson to learn from this is *always give a considered response.* Not just to allegations like this, but also, for example, if a parent or colleague or pupil seeks your advice on something. It is easy to 'shoot from the hip' and react quickly – and badly. Much better to offer an initial non-committal but sympathetic response then take an hour or two (or even a day or two) to reflect, consider the facts and the possible range of responses *before you actually respond.* Avoid responding when emotions are running high.

Honesty is the best policy

If you make a mistake, never try to hide it from your headteacher or line manager. Chances are, if you confess, you will be supported, whereas if you disguise it, it will come back to sink its teeth into your derrière. Professionally speaking, that is. This is most apparent when things go wrong with parents.

brilliant example

A teacher, in the midst of 'telling off' a particularly recalcitrant Year 6 boy, prodded him in the chest with her finger to emphasise what she was saying. The boy said he intended to tell his mum because, 'teachers aren't allowed to touch children'. Which was entirely true.

This uncharacteristic loss of temper had taken the teacher by surprise and she now saw her entire future career ruined because of this lapse. She could have tried to hide it – her word against the boy's – but was not at all comfortable lying. She decided to go straight to her headteacher and explain.

'I'm afraid I lost my temper when Ryan thumped another younger child and, as I told him off, I prodded my finger in his chest. Several times. I'm sorry. It's not something I've done before or would do again.'

The headteacher admired the teacher's honesty and bravery and was also grateful to be forewarned before the potentially angry parent arrived. The headteacher, instead, contacted the parent first, explained how the teacher's lapse was unacceptable and explained how the parent might make a formal complaint. The headteacher added that the parent did not have to take this route if she was satisfied that the matter had been dealt with satisfactorily.

The parent recognised the problems her own child presented to any school, was grateful to the headteacher for being honest and was happy, on this occasion, to let the matter lie, providing the teacher apologised to her son. Thus the situation was resolved amicably, principally because the teacher had taken prompt action following the lapse.

brilliant tip

List your achievements. Chances are the list is more lengthy and substantial than you might have thought. This is an especially good thing to do when you are feeling despondent, feeling that you are working hard without achieving much. These can also be kept as notes for any applications you are about to make.

Summary

Brilliant teachers can be fulfilled staying in a class-based role for their entire career, providing they remain motivated, interested and open to the possibility of change and development.

Seeking promotion is a desirable option for many, but always make sure you choose your moves very carefully to maximise the likelihood of success. Some teachers' careers have halted or failed as a result of making an unwise choice of job and setting.

We all make mistakes. Be honest about them, learn from them and avoid repeating them. Hiding mistakes is the biggest mistake of all.

As someone famously noted in a malapropism, as a brilliant teacher, the world is your lobster!

Afterword

You, dear reader, have either read through every word in this book and will, hopefully, have benefited from the advice herein (even if you may not agree with all of it) or, you may be browsing through it in a corner of a bookshop wondering how it ends. In which case, slap yourself on the wrist for your impatience, pay the cover price and read it properly. It's not a whodunnit.

Much of the information I have attempted to impart is good, common sense. Some of it is more arcane, gleaned from years of hard-won experience and designed to save you the time, effort and inconvenience of experiencing it in the old-fashioned and time-consuming manner of actually living it.

The lasting impression I hope I have left you with is the sheer, wanton enjoyability of being a brilliant primary school teacher. Some jobs are equally (and, occasionally, more) demanding, but no other job allows you to influence for the better so many people – people who will themselves go on to live in and shape tomorrow's world, people who have learned from you some of the most valuable and life-enhancing lessons they will ever learn.

Look around the crowded city centre, the airport, the football crowd – anywhere that large numbers of people gather. Think of how each and every one of those people has had several teachers who have helped make them the person they are. Think of how the vast majority of them are well-rounded, responsible members of society. Think of the range of their occupations,

their interests and their talents, the immense and varied contributions each of them makes to the society in which they live.
Think, too, of the less content amongst them – those whose
lives may have been transformed for the better had they had the
advantage of having had a brilliant teacher. Think of all this and
tell me, hand on heart, that you are not excited by the possibility
of playing your part.

The classic teaching movie is *Goodbye, Mr. Chips!* – a tale of a
fuddy-duddy chap who finds, almost to his surprise, that he
transforms lives for the better in his role as a teacher. On his
death bed, when one in attendance whispers, 'What a shame
he never had any children!' the seraphically smiling (but soon-
to-be-late) Mr Chips demurs, 'Oh, but I did have children.
Hundreds of them!' You could have hundreds yourself, with the
indubitable advantage that, at the end of each day, you can hand
them back to their parents for at least 17 hours. Years after they
have left your class, you may have the pleasure of meeting them
and they will beam and shake your hand, tell you how they loved
being in your class and how you made such a difference to their
lives. It happens to brilliant primary teachers frequently. And,
believe me, it feels great.

So the next time the photocopier breaks down, the computer
crashes, the irate parent looms in your classroom doorway, or the
intractable 'behaviourally challenged' child does something else
that is likely to raise your blood pressure, just remember how
lucky you are to be in the best job in the world.

Further reading

(All titles published by Pearson)

Barron, P. *Classroom Gems: Games, Ideas and Activities for Learning Outside the Primary Classroom.*

Barron, P. *Classroom Gems: Practical Ideas, Games and Activities for the Primary Classroom.*

Dix, P. *The Essential Guide to Classroom Assessment.*

Dix, P. *The Essential Guide to Taking Care of Behaviour.*

Haigh, A. *The Art of Teaching.*

Trant, J. *The Essential Guide to Successful School Trips: Practical Skills for Teachers.*

Walker, L. *The Essential Guide to Lesson Planning.*

Index